Growing up in
THE FIRST WORLD WAR

Renée Huggett

Batsford Academic and Educational   London

Typeset by Tek-Art Ltd, Kent
and printed in Great Britain by
R.J. Acford
Chichester, Sussex
for the publishers
Batsford Academic and Educational,
an imprint of B.T. Batsford Ltd,
4 Fitzhardinge Street
London W1H 0AH

ISBN 0 7134 4773 7

Acknowledgments

The Author and Publishers would like to thank the
following for their kind permission to use copyright
illustrations in this book: Robert Beard for figures
41, 52, 54 and 55; Pauline Challender for figure 17;
Christies for figures 38 and 39; Dartington Rural
Archive for figure 44; Imperial War Museum for
figures 5, 7, 9, 11, 12, 13, 14, 15, 18, 19, 20, 24, 25, 26,
27, 31, 42, 43, 45, 46, 47, 48, 49, 53, 56, 57, 58, 59 and
60; London Borough of Camden for figures 28, 29
and 50; London Borough of Hackney for figures 4,
16 and 51; Dorothy Yeoman for figures 1, 2, 8 and
36. The Author would also like to thank the
Salvation Army; the NSPCC, who allowed her to
use its archives; the Rev. Mair of Thurston, Suffolk,
for his help and advice; and all the people who
allowed her to interview them and whose
experiences appear throughout this book.

Contents

The Illustrations

1 How It Began

One sunny morning in June 1914, Archduke Franz Ferdinand and his wife Sophie were riding in an open car through the streets of Sarajevo in the little country of Bosnia (now Yugoslavia). Although he was heir to the throne of the great Austro-Hungarian empire, Franz Ferdinand was not popular in his own country. He was a vain, domineering man and, even worse, he had married someone who was only a countess. Because she was not of royal blood, she was considered unsuitable to marry into the proud Habsburg dynasty. As a result, his wife was not allowed to sit beside him at any of the great banquets or on other State occasions.

But Franz Ferdinand, who had married for love, was proud of his wife and wanted her to share in the official splendours of his life. So, on the anniversary of his wedding day he had brought Sophie to Bosnia to inspect the army. At least there she could sit beside him as the wife of the Inspector General of the Austro-Hungarian army.

But, if he was disliked at home, Franz Ferdinand was even more unpopular in Bosnia, which had been annexed by the Austro-Hungarian empire only six years before, in 1908. Many of the inhabitants were Serbs who wanted Bosnia to become part of the adjacent country of Serbia. When it was learnt that Franz Ferdinand was to visit Sarajevo, a small group of students decided to assassinate him. As the royal car entered the town, one of the students threw a bomb; it missed the car, but killed some of the bystanders.

When Franz Ferdinand arrived at the Town Hall, he angrily decided to cancel the inspection and drive straight out of town. But his chauffeur took the wrong turning and stopped the car near a bridge, so that he could reverse. One of the would-be assassins, who happened to be standing nearby, saw his opportunity, sprang on to the running board of the car and fired point blank at Franz Ferdinand and his wife. They both died almost immediately. The assassin, 19-year-old Gavrilo Princip, was arrested and charged with the murders. (He escaped the death sentence because he was under 21, but he died in prison of consumption within a few years.)

That incident sparked off the fuse which exploded into the First World War.

1   At the end of the bridge at Sarajevo where Gavrilo Princip is supposed to have stood when he assassinated the Archduke Franz Ferdinand and his wife, footprints have been set in concrete.

Very few people in Britain, however, had ever heard of Bosnia. It was far away in the Balkans. Many newspapers reported the assassination only briefly, and some did not mention it at all. But, behind the scenes, in embassies and consulates, there was great activity. Letters and telegrams were sent. Most of the heads of state were on holiday, so communications were slow. But within five weeks, most of Europe was at war.

Just as some people today fear that a small incident could set off a nuclear holocaust, it needed only that single event in 1914 to bring to a head all the international rivalries, hatreds and fears which lay beneath the surface.

Austria had had trouble with Serbia before. After receiving a promise of support from Germany, the Austrians sent an ultimatum to Serbia, making impossible demands. Russia, as the champion of her fellow Slavs in the Balkans, promised Serbia her support.

War comes

When Serbia refused to accept all of the Austrian demands, Austria declared war on her on 28 July. The following day, Russia started to mobilize. Germany then declared war on Russia in support of Austria and, two days later, on France, after the latter had begun to mobilize in support of her ally, Russia. And, when German forces marched through the neutral country of Belgium to attack France, Britain declared war on

Germany – on 4 August, 1914. The war, which was to cost Britain 750,000 lives and another 1,750,000 wounded, had begun.

3 This picture, taken at the beginning of the war, reflects the peaceful England which was to vanish for ever. Looking out across the Channel, could they see the war clouds gathering over France? During that last bank holiday no one believed that war would begin.

2 Your Country Needs You

It had been a long, hot summer. By the beginning of August some lucky children of wealthy parents were already playing in the grounds of their vast estates in the country or riding their ponies through the parks and forests. Some children were staying in large hotels or rented mansions in select British holiday resorts on the Norfolk and Sussex coasts or even abroad, in France. Others were at camps organized by the Boy Scouts, the Boys' Brigade, or other organizations. But, for the majority of children, there was no holiday. They stayed at home and many country lads of 12 or 13 spent their whole school holiday working out in the fields to bring in the harvest on horse-drawn wagons for five shillings (25p) a week.

The best that most children could ever look forward to was a cheap day's excursion by rail to a seaside resort on Bank Holiday Monday. The *Coventry Herald* advertised excursions on the London and North Western Railway to Blackpool for six shillings (30p) and to Bournemouth for 13 shillings (65p).

Bank Holiday weekend, which started on Saturday, 1 August, was particularly fine and sunny but it was overshadowed by the looming war clouds in Europe. On that day, the *Kentish Gazette*, which had failed to report the assassination of Franz Ferdinand, had a headline WAR NOW INEVITABLE. It revealed that Russia had already mobilized 1,200,000 troops and that Germany and Austria were lining up against Britain.

The declaration of war
Families went ahead with their Bank Holiday plans. Children cheered at a firework display in Crystal Palace, London, as portraits of George V and Queen Mary glittered in the night sky, while a band played the National Anthem. But there was an increasing sense of tension – and excitement – in the air as the street placards of newspaper vendors spelled out the approach of war: GERMAN INVASION OF BELGIUM.

Up to that time it had not been absolutely certain that Britain, which had not taken part in any Continental war since Napoleonic times, would be involved, but her guarantee of Belgian neutrality made conflict inevitable.

On 2 August the Labour party organized anti-war demonstrations and on the day war was declared, the *Daily Herald* warned:

> We need peace; we must have peace; our children will thank us if we make possible the realisation of its promise.

But these were still small voices of protest.

Almost everyone was excited by the prospect of war. Huge crowds, including many children, gathered in London outside Buckingham Palace, just as similar crowds were assembling in other capitals throughout Europe.

With no radios or televisions people had to rely on newspapers or word of mouth to discover that the war had started. One young man, who later wrote a book about the First World War, found out in a different way:

> As we climbed the hill to the Verne about 8 am I noticed a Red Cross flag flying from the Naval hospital flagstaff at Portland and

4 This man was suspected of being a pacifist and was chased and jeered at by the crowd. Often the police had to be called for protection because Kitchener's propaganda had convinced many people that war was the patriotic solution. By the end of the war, most of the soldiers in the trenches had changed their minds.

so I knew that war had been declared. (Medical Officer of HM 23rd Foot, Royal Welsh Fusiliers, *The War the Infantry Knew*, P.S. King & Son Ltd 1938)

Esme Strachey (born 1902) remembers that she heard about it while she was staying with her grandmother in a house on Wimbledon Common.

She had rented it for the summer from Arding and Hobbs, a drapers' shop. There were palms and marble statues in the hall. My mother was just remarrying so I expect was occupied with other thoughts.

But this was exceptional. Most people were gripped by war fever and hatred of the Germans. Esme Strachey again:

We had some German relations who were very unpopular with my family. Everyone said the Kaiser was a devil.

New money
To prevent a run on savings, the holiday had been extended for a day and, when the banks re-opened, customers were presented with crisp, new pound notes instead of real gold sovereigns. But the queues at banks were much shorter than those at army recruiting centres.

Army volunteers
In all parts of the country, men flocked to the centres, hoping to get into the fight against the "Hun" before the war ended. "My parents," said Ann Vincent (born 1908), "thought that the war would be over by Christmas." It was a common sentiment. Unlike other European countries, Britain did not have a conscript army, so it was essential to get volunteers.

Huge recruiting posters were put up on hoardings, walls, and at railway stations all over the country. All children who lived through the First World War remember the most famous one of all, showing the Minister of War, Lord Kitchener, with his heavy, handlebar moustache and pointing finger, and a simple caption: "Your Country Needs You".

His advice to recruits, which they were urged to keep safely in their pay books was:

> *Drink:* Don't! Hot or cold tea.
> *Sore feet:* Keep your feet hard and your boots soft.
> *Cleanliness:* Clean bodies, clean food, clean drink.

This advice was somewhat difficult to observe in the mud and squalor of the trenches on the Western Front.

Parades
Military bands paraded in the streets and young children soon took up the call themselves, using old saucepans and wooden boxes for drums and sticks for swords, marching along behind the adult soldiers. Passers-by often threw them halfpennies as a reward for their patriotism.

Initial training
The authorities were so overwhelmed by the

5 Posters were so much a part of the Great War ▶ that many of them are still famous today. This one is Australian but every country was asking God for help in destroying "the enemy" and for looking after each husband or daddy.

influx of recruits into the army – half a million in the first month of the war – that they could neither clothe nor equip them.

A territorial, who had been called up the day after war was declared, wrote in his diary for 15 August:

> I went over to Woolwich one day this week to have a look round. All over the parched grass of the common, squads of men in civilian clothes were being drilled by NCOs in khaki, in the dust and the sunshine. (Anon, *A Soldier's Diary*)

A similar scene was being repeated on commons and in parks all over Britain, with recruits in civilian clothes drilling with pieces of lead pipe or walking sticks instead of rifles and whirring wooden rattles instead of firing machine guns.

Young children thought it was a wonderful game and played at being soldiers alongside the recruits, though as *The Times* noted on 10 March, 1915, these children "for all their set faces and stalwart bodies seem still pitifully young".

God bless dear Daddy who is fighting the Hun and send him **Help**

ISSUED BY THE GOVERNMENT OF THE COMMONWEALTH OF AUSTRALIA.   W. E. SMITH. LTD. SYDNEY

6 These young men were in the territorial army formed by Lord Haldane in 1906. When the war started, they provided a highly-trained force of seven divisions. Within a few weeks of the outbreak of war, they were fighting in France.

To stem the flood of recruits it couldn't cope with, the army raised the minimum height standard on 11 September, 1914, from 5 feet 3 inches – and a 34 inch chest – to 5 feet 6 inches. But later, when the casualties on the Western Front began to mount alarmingly, they had to reduce the height to 5 feet 3 inches again.

Under-age recruits

Men were not allowed to enlist until they were 19, but many lads tried to join up when they were younger. Recruiting sergeants, who got a bonus for each recruit, sometimes turned a blind eye to their real age. One young lad of 16, who was foolish enough to give his correct age, was told by the sergeant: "You come back again tomorrow, sonny. See how old you are then." When the boy returned the following day and said he was 19, he was immediately accepted. "You've grown up now," the sergeant laughed.

Other recruiting sergeants were said to roam the cinemas and music-halls looking for 15- or 16-year-old boys who looked older than their age and who might be persuaded to enlist. If they did so, they were given the King's shilling (5p) which was all that private soldiers were paid per day in 1914.

Much younger boys – of 12 or 13 – managed to get into the army. In 1916, the *Daily Mirror* published a picture of a private soldier who joined a regiment when he was 12 and had served for six weeks on the Western Front before his true age was discovered and he was discharged.

Some under-age volunteers were wounded. Herbert Bell (born 1897) joined up when he was 18. After serving in India and the Middle East, he was shipped over to Marseilles in 1918 and travelled across France by troop train to the Western Front. He was in the front line for 12 days and left for a period of rest before returning to the trenches on 19 July, 1918. His brief war-time diary describes what happened next.

July 19 Left in motors through Germain to join Battalion. Met them late in afternoon, outside Rheims Wood. That night proceeded with Company through woods and went into action next morning.

July 20 9 a.m. Went over the top [of the trench, in order to attack the enemy]. I was sent on as scout and went through Rheims Wood all right and came to the end and was just going out into corn field when I was wounded, about 9.15 a.m. Got back to trench that afternoon and managed to get back to Field Dressing Station by dinner time, and got to Field Ambulance about 4 p.m. Here noticed several of the old boys.

July 22 Reached Rouen 5 General Hospital. Here went through operation and had bullet taken out of my back. It had gone down through my left shoulder.

July 26 Left Rouen for Southampton.

Tom Wills (born 1899) joined up when he was 17. He was sent over to France and towards the end of the war he was wounded in both legs.

I was sent to a hospital in Boulogne. Then I was brought back to England in a hospital

7   Young boys in a recruiting office at the beginning of the war.

8 As the war went on, it became necessary not only to introduce conscription but also to recruit older men who had retired. This man, an army sergeant, became a trainer of the young recruits.

ship. We had two ships and an air ship to protect us.

A number of under-age recruits were killed. The *Chislehurst and District Times* reported on 3 September, 1915, that William Beckington who had joined up at the age of 17 had been killed by a shot through the head.

Sylvia Pankhurst, the famous suffragette reported an even more tragic case of an East End Jewish boy who had joined up without his parents' knowledge or consent in September 1914, when he was only just 18. Later, in January 1916, they received an official letter saying that their son had been wounded and shocked by a mine explosion. They had several letters from their son and on 23 February, 1916, there was one from him saying:

> We were in the trenches and I was ill, so I went out and they took me to the prison and I am in a bit of trouble now. I will have to go in front of a Court.

Then there were no more letters until, on 8 April, a curt official letter arrived:

> Sir,
> I am directed to inform you that a report has been received from the War Office to the effect that Private . . . was sentenced after trial by court martial to suffer death by being shot for desertion and the sentence was duly executed on March 20 1916.
> (Sylvia Pankhurst, *The Home Front*)

Although under-age recruits could be imprisoned for giving a false age, they continued to enlist. It was not always possible to make them produce a birth certificate as the registration of births was not made compulsory until 1915.

Army cadets

For those younger lads who couldn't wait to get into uniform, there was always the cadet corps which were run by most regiments. The First Cadet Battalion, the Royal Fusiliers, took "smart lads" of 14 years of age upwards, who were physically fit and over 5 feet 2 inches in height, and provided them with a uniform consisting of a khaki cap, tunic, trousers,

9 Naval cadets training at the Nautical College, queueing at the tuck shop. These boys were being trained to become officers.

putties, black lace-up boots, belts, pouch and frog. Their walking-out order consisted of service dress without pouch or frog and a swagger cane to be carried.

In the evenings they were given a full training in drill, shooting, stretcher-bearing, communications and other military arts, so that by the time they transferred to the army they were much better equipped than other recruits.

There was also an annual inspection; week-end training when cadets were advised to bring sufficient rations for two meals of bread and cheese, boiled eggs and meat; and an annual week's camp with sports, drill and a torchlight tattoo. Cadets had to pay seven shillings (35p) towards their expenses, which could be paid by instalments.

Some of their Field days did not work out quite as intended. On 16 July 1916, they had an encounter with Haberdashers' School Cadet Corps on Hampstead Heath. The Battalion magazine reported:

> After an unfortunate mistake as to the whereabouts of the enemy, which occasioned much vicious charging at trees, hedges and cliffs, and a thorough exploration of a large area of woodland, we had an exciting charge into a bog, followed by a strenuous struggle with certain of the defenders.

By 1916, some 1400 cadets from the Battalion had gone into the Forces – and many of them were already dead, like Drummer A.C. Riley. The Battalion magazine for January 1916 noted:

> We have lost one of the best for duty and the life of the drums.

10 Family and personal photographs are very much a part of the Great War. Every soldier on enlistment had his photograph taken for display in the front room, and pictures like this one became treasured possessions. This might be the last time they would all be together.

Horses

It wasn't only men who were needed in France, but horses, too, to draw wagonloads of rations and munitions up to the front line at night and for field ambulances carrying the sick or wounded back to field or base hospitals. So, all over the country, the army requisitioned horses from farmers, tradesmen, and private stables.

Coastal towns

The coastal ports were also extremely busy. Jack Vincent (born 1905) remembers the Royal Naval Reserve being called up in Looe, Cornwall, which included a great number of local fishermen.

They were instructed to muster on the sea front. A few had already had a celebration drink or two and quite a few had been wearing their uniform trousers whilst fishing. So they weren't quite a spick and span contingent when they fell in to board the train to Plymouth.

3 Over There

The British Expeditionary Force had its first encounter with the Germans at Mons, south of Brussels on 23 August, but was forced to retreat in the face of superior numbers. As the German army crossed the Belgian border and swept on towards Paris, the British and French troops were pressed back across the rivers Aisne and Marne. Eventually, the Allies managed to hold a line and start beating the Germans back towards the rivers again.

Battle of the Marne

The Battle of the Marne was a terrifying experience for children caught in the firing line.

Raymonde Butcher (born 1899) married an Englishman when she grew up. As a girl, she lived in Vertus just south of the River Marne.

> Our village was right in the front line. We saw the French army coming through, going to the battle, hundreds of marching soldiers, and then they were retreating. The men looked so tired, it was thought they would be unable to fight.
>
> People had to leave their houses for the battle. Some people left the village for ever.
>
> We could see the shells. Some people lived in the cellars, but we didn't. During the battle, there was a lull. The French were hidden in the ditches. Everything was quiet. We went to bed. We were awakened and they were fighting in the yard. It was terrible. Hand to hand fighting with bayonets. In the evening, we heard steps and looked out and it was the Germans. We used to peep through the crack in the shutters.
>
> Later on, they banged the door and asked if they could stay. My mother said there was no room and they left.
>
> But if the houses were empty, they just broke down the doors. There was one big empty house and the Germans took the contents and drank the wine.
>
> During the battle the Germans took charge of the shops so that the food was distributed fairly.

11 This is the desolate landscape in which many ▶ of the battles were fought. It is 1916, so those little houses were lucky still to be there. The typical British notice about horses sounds rather strange when it is remembered that these same horses were being ridden into battle and injured and killed in their thousands.

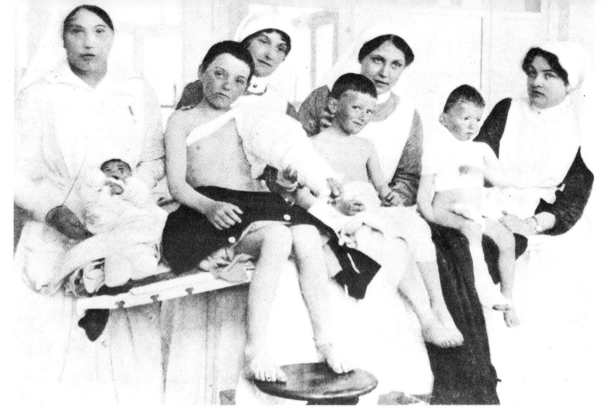

12　A baby is amongst the injured in this hospital. The children in Europe experienced war at first hand and became accustomed to the sound of shells and guns firing day and night.

Then as the Germans pushed on south of the village, we saw our young soldiers coming back as prisoners. They had to march with the Germans. There were wounded prisoners. They walked, too. They took them all back to Germany.

A woman passing was carrying two baskets of apples. The soldiers fell on the apples, so she went back for more.

Later on, when the French won the next battle, we had French soldiers coming back through the village again.

Raymonde Butcher was lucky to survive the battle unhurt, but other children were not so fortunate. The fighting in Soissons on the river Aisne was particularly fierce and was preceded by a massive German bombardment. Terrified children crouched with their mothers in the cellars as the German shells burst in the town, knocking houses to the ground.

One French woman told how the next-door house was struck by a shell and reduced to ruins. The 13-year-old daughter of the house was killed instantly. Another little girl in a nearby house had her arm cut off by a fragment of shell, while another neighbour's boy also lost a limb. The woman saw a soldier in the street outside walking along fit and well, and the next moment he was struck by a fragment of shell which hurled his head against the wall opposite.

The plight of innocent babies and children did not leave the hearts of soldiers untouched. Bombardier Stoddard of the Royal Artillery, recounted how one day he heard a cry from an empty house.

When I went in I found a baby, about eleven months old, lying crying in its night-gown. I brought the youngster out.

It was raining in torrents at the time, and I carried it about five and a half miles.

It was crying all the way, and I tried to conceal it from our sergeant, but eventually he said I should be obliged to put it down as we were going into action, so I laid it in a hedge and covered it with some straw, hoping that someone would soon find it and take care of it. It made me think of my own children. (*The War Stories of Private Thomas Atkins*, George Newnes Ltd, 1914)

Eastern Front

The experiences of children on the Eastern Front were even worse than those of children on the Western Front; warfare there was much more mobile, with huge armies attacking and counter-attacking on wide fronts hundreds of miles in depth.

When war broke out, the Russian army, which totalled over seven million men in all, swept across the borders of the Austro-Hungarian empire. They were eventually pushed back but went on the offensive again in 1916 under the command of General Brusilov. In the following year, widespread desertions from the Russian army, which preceded the Russian revolution of 1917, allowed the Austro-German forces to make deep penetrations into Russian territory again.

One of the millions of children who suffered on the Eastern Front was Zara Hershman (born 1910), who has lived in Britain since 1919.

I was born in Austria, so I was on the other side. The month the war started my mother had another baby, so there were then five children. My father was in England on business when war broke out, so we didn't see him again till after the war.

When the Russians advanced, we had to run away.

My mother took the baby in her arms and we decided to make our way to a safe spot. We could not get into a train. They were all full of people fleeing from the Russian enemy.

We walked and walked until we had no soles on our shoes.

That evening when it got dark we got to a village. Someone said, "tomorrow morning a caravan is going through". We slept and started in time to get the bus. We got to a point, but couldn't go on, so we decided to go back home.

The Russians had been through and burnt most of the town including our house.

Just outside the town there was a small wood and the shell of a little house. It had a cellar and we sheltered there.

We had no food. My sister was about 12 years of age and she went out to the fields where the new potatoes had been sown and she grubbed out the potatoes that were underneath with her bare hands. We used to make a fire and roast potatoes.

One day a Russian soldier took pity on her and gave her a hunk of bread.

We contacted my grandmother who had a flat in Vienna and she suggested that we should join her there.

On the way, we and some other refugees had to go through a forest. Suddenly we heard a sound of hooves. Two Cossacks came along. We could not understand Russian but they made us understand. We stood in a row as they indicated. They took coils of ropes and opened them and showed they were going to hang us. We were all terrified. Everyone screamed and cried.

Then they took out their swords and showed they were going to cut all our throats. We all screamed again.

Then they just rode off through the trees, laughing, and left us. They were just having fun at our expense; but it is something you never forget.

Trench warfare

Millions of children had similar, unforgettable, terrifying experiences on the fluid Eastern Front. But after the initial movements in Belgium and the Battle of the Marne, the fighting on the Western Front congealed into a static, bloody confrontation.

13 Throughout the war, dogs were used to carry messages to the soldiers in the trenches. Around their necks are the cylinders in which the messages were carried. ·

14 Some of the worst battles of the war took place around Ypres. These children were wounded by German shells and are being taken in these "basket" stretchers to the hospital.

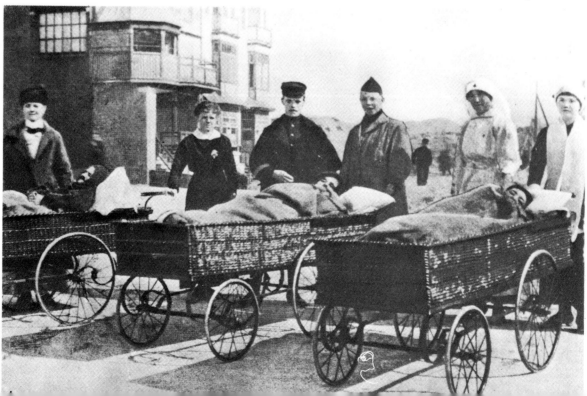

A line of trenches stretched from the Belgian coast to the Swiss border, separated on average by about 350 yards of "No Man's Land" – a barren wilderness of mud, barbed wire, shell craters, branchless trees and rotting corpses.

The children in these areas learnt to live with the daily sight of young, fresh-faced recruits marching up to the trenches and the walking wounded shuffling back, the neat whiteness of the bandages around their foreheads contrasting sharply with their drawn, grimy faces. The children also learnt to live with the deafening thunder of the guns and the ominous silence which preceded another foredoomed attack across No-Man's Land. It was like living at the gates of hell. Raymonde Butcher (born 1899):

> We heard the guns all day and night. There were soldiers all the time. I only saw the trenches afterwards. Every house in Rheims was damaged. The cathedral was burnt. It was a soldiers' war.

Private Knede of the Liverpool Regiment describes a typical week in the trenches.

> It was a thousand times worse than being in hell. For six days we were in the same trenches, almost at arm's reach of the enemy. We could only steal out under cover of darkness for a drink of water.
>
> It rained all the time; but we had to make the best of it. Everyday was the same as the day before – an advance at daybreak and at night; but every time we were beaten back by frightful odds. Each time we were forced back we left hundreds of our men behind, killed and wounded.

Day after day, every minute during the day, German shells were falling around us like rain. We could hear them coming through the air and we would lie low in the trenches and say "That is another one that has missed us".

But the fatal one came without us hearing it. Thirteen of us were together and only one lucky devil escaped. When the blow came I thought my head was taken off.

I fell on my knees and put one arm up in the air, and said, "Good God, is this death?" I then put my hand on my face, and I felt the flesh which was so badly torn. But I felt no pain. I seemed dead.

I crept along the top of the trenches until I found the doctor who was with my regiment. He simply put a piece of cotton wool over my face and laid me under a tree, as the firing was too heavy to get a proper dressing on.

For five hours I lay bleeding under that tree and the German shells were still falling about us like rain. (*The War Stories of Private Thomas Atkins*)

Gas attacks

A new dimension of horror was added to trench warfare in April 1915 at Ypres when the Germans used gas, which left its ashen-faced victims spluttering for breath and frothing at the mouth, until they died up to two days later.

15 Rheims was always near the front line throughout the war. The schools were still open, but the children always had to be prepared. Gas was first used in the trenches in 1915 after which all children were given gas masks.

Recruiting meetings

Yet volunteers continued to come forward at an average of 100,000 a month, urged on by a variety of reasons: patriotism, hatred of the "Hun", a sense of duty, horror at German atrocities in Belgium, love of adventure, unemployment, and social pressures from friends, family, wives, sweethearts, neighbours.

Some houses had notices in their front windows proclaiming how many sons were serving on the Western Front. Herbert Bell (born 1897) had his photograph taken as soon as he got into uniform. His mother proudly displayed it on the mantelpiece in the front room – just as other mothers were doing all over the country.

In all the main cities there were constant recruiting meetings with martial music being played by bands or through the brass horns of wind-up gramophones.

Women were the best unpaid recruiting sergeants. Young girls and old women roamed the city streets giving a white feather, signifying cowardice, to any likely-looking lads not wearing uniform, which could include any tall, well-built school boy who looked older than his years.

16 An armoured tank in London, being used as a platform at one of the recruiting meetings which continued throughout the war. Tanks were also used as a kind of "office" for selling war bonds and certificates to raise money for the war.

With its impish sense of humour, *Punch* published a delightful cartoon by Frank Reynolds, showing a fat, short-sighted old lady, dressed entirely in black, peering disapprovingly at a cardboard cut-out of Charlie Chaplin outside a cinema, and observing that a couple of months in the army would make a new man of him.

But the activities of these voluntary recruiting sergeants sometimes had tragic consequences. Mary Taylor (born 1898) says:

I had a cousin in the merchant navy who always stayed with us when they docked in the Thames. They had no uniforms and he got so fed up with being given white feathers by stupid women that he joined the army, which he hated. He was sent off to the trenches and was killed within a week.

Conscription

The volunteer system, which produced three

17 The world war was fought not only in European countries, but also in Asia, and the Middle East. These children are Armenians in the Jelus Refugee Camp at Baqubah, where the Allies were fighting against the Turks. It was during this war that refugees began to create a world problem which is still with us today.

million recruits in all, produced unequal sacrifices, but the Liberals in the coalition government were strongly opposed to conscription.

It was not introduced until 1916, when losses on the Western Front were increasing at an alarming rate. The Battle of the Somme in that year resulted in nearly half a million British casualties. Alice Hancox (born 1897) says of this battle:

> When they gave our soldiers the order to go, the Germans were waiting for them. It was terrible.

But the slaughter still went on – at Arras, 150,000 casualties, at Passchendale, another 250,000 – right up to the end of the war.

4 The Home Front

The war, which was always called the Great War at the time, had a much bigger impact on children's lives than any previous conflict. In the past, unless their father was a soldier or a sailor, children were scarcely affected, but no one at home could escape the consequences of this war.

Young children woke up at night, terrified by the distant rumbling of the artillery barrage in France and Flanders, which was often so intense that it could be plainly heard in the south-eastern corner of England.

But there were much more direct consequences. For the first time ever, civilian lives came under attack from the air.

Flying machines

Aviation was still in its infancy. Count von

18   A German naval airship.

Zepplin, a German army officer built the first airship, a 420-feet long, sausage-shaped dirigible, in 1900. Three years later, the two Wright brothers made the first flight in an aeroplane – for all of 12 seconds. In 1909, a Frenchman, Louis Bleriot, flew across the English Channel in a primitive monoplane.

But, in 1914, few children had ever seen a Zeppelin or an aircraft, unless it was Bleriot's plane which had been displayed to excited crowds in Selfridge's store in London. The war was to give them a chance to make a closer acquaintance and, for many, it was too close for comfort.

The blackout

A few weeks after the outbreak of war, the Government, fearing Zeppelin raids, ordered streets lights to be dimmed. Most of these were still gas lights, which had to be turned on by a lamplighter with a long pole. The top and sides of the lamps were painted black so that only a narrow cone of light was cast down to the pavement.

Careless children who forgot to pull their curtains at night would be shouted at by constables specially assigned to patrol the streets. But as many houses had only thin or badly fitting curtains – and some in the slums had none at all – the black-out was not very effective, particularly as the bright lights from munitions factories and blast furnaces still blazed into the night sky.

First air raids

The first attacks were made, not by Zeppelins, but by planes, which dropped a few bombs harmlessly around Dover in December 1914. The following month two Zeppelins dropped over 20 bombs on Great Yarmouth and King's Lynn, Norfolk, killing four people and injuring another 16. There were half a dozen other raids before London was bombed at the end of May 1915. Seven people in the East End were killed and 35 injured.

Children used to shelter under kitchen tables, under the stairs or even under ripped-up floorboards during the raids. Sidney Offord (born 1908), who lived in London, recalls:

> We used to go and sit in the basement, not at the bottom, but on the stairs.

There were no public air-raid shelters, though some richer families had the cellars and the basements of their homes reinforced by sandbags. Other families also took their own air-raid precautions. Rose Greaves (born 1908) who lived in Morley, near Leeds, says:

> I had some cousins in Harringay. They used to put a pail of water at the bottom of the stairs and a pail of water at the top in case there was an air raid and a fire.

During daylight raids, Boy Scouts used to cycle round the streets with placards reading "take cover" or "all clear". Maroons, to warn civilians of impending air raids, were not installed in London until 1917.

At first, children were more fascinated than frightened by the air raids. They rushed out into the streets whenever a Zeppelin passed over.

Most of London's children seem to have been out in the streets in the early hours of 3 September, 1916, when a German airship was caught by the thin, bright fingers of the searchlights, weaving across the sky.

Mary Taylor (born 1898) who lived in Hampstead says:

> Mother woke us all one night to see the

19   A London family looking at their home which had been demolished in an air raid in October 1915.

> Zeppelin pass over, lit by searchlights. It was a marvellous sight.

She watched, fascinated, as the airship turned away, still clearly illuminated by the searchlights, with shells from the anti-aircraft guns bursting all around it. Suddenly all the searchlights snapped off. And a few minutes later, the airship could be seen again, with small tongues of flame licking at its sides before it burst into a brilliant crimson fireball in the air. A great cheer rose up from all the children watching in the streets, while their parents kissed and hugged each other.

The airship, which was not actually a Zeppelin but a similar machine of a different make, was the first to be destroyed over England. The pilot who shot it down, second Lieutenant Leefe Robinson of the Royal Flying Corps became a national hero overnight and was given a V.C. (the highest award for gallantry) a few days later.

The airship had come down in the village of Cuffley, Hertfordshire. Later that Sunday morning, thousands of children streamed out of London to see the wreckage. But not all of them were lucky enough to find it. Mary Taylor (born 1898) recalls:

> Two friends and I walked next day – the

trams were all full – to see the remains, but found nothing. I think we worked it out that we had walked 16 miles.

The wreckage was later exhibited in a marquee in London with all the proceeds going to war charities.

Air raids produced a craze among boys for collecting pieces of shrapnel from anti-aircraft shells. They swapped ·fragments from their collections. The most treasured item was a nose cap. Despite the intense anti-aircraft barrage, shrapnel was not always easy to find. Sidney Offord (born 1908) says:

> One night we heard a terrible thump. The next day I found a charred piece of metal. I took it to school but the master laughed and said it was a falling meteorite. I thought it was a piece of shrapnel.
>
> The streets were made of wooden blocks. We suddenly noticed that these blocks had bits of steel in them. We took these out, thinking it was shrapnel, but they were from motor cars. Bits often fell off cars in those days.

Raids by planes

As British pilots and gunners became more

20 The number of orphans naturally increased during the war. There was little public provision for such vast numbers and it was mainly charitable bodies who tried to help them. This lady has taken some war orphans on an outing to her manor house where they are taking part in a skipping race.

successful in bringing down the Zeppelins, the Germans started to use bomber planes instead: Gotha biplanes, with bombs under the wings, and a top speed of 80 m.p.h.

Children's attitudes towards air raids changed as more people were killed or injured. During the first daylight raid by Gothas on London, a bomb crashed through three floors of a school in Poplar before exploding on the ground floor, where it killed 15 children and wounded 30 others.

Although London and the South-East suffered the worst attacks, many other parts of the country were raided. Rose Greaves (born 1908) who lived in a Yorkshire mill town says:

> There were two Zeppelin raids. I was very frightened, but I think that was more towards the end of the war.

Richer parents took their children away

from London. Esme Strachey went to North Wales to be away from it. But most of the cockneys in the East End, which suffered some of the worst attacks, had nowhere else to go.

Despite official opposition, thousands of children and their parents flocked into Underground stations and tunnels under the Thames at night and resisted all attempts by police to remove them.

In comparison with the Second World War, air raid casualties were small – nearly 1400 killed and over 3300 injured – but it was the first time in history that women and children had been deliberately attacked from the air.

Anti-German riots

These "baby-killer" raids, as they were called, provoked great anger in Britain. Although many Germans and Austrians had been interned on the outbreak of war, those who had been naturalized remained at liberty and others found it relatively easy to escape internment.

The father of Zara Hershman (born 1910) had come over from his native Austria on business just before the outbreak of war.

He was an enemy alien, but he was never interned. He knew a lot about wood, so he went to a timber mill and asked if he could buy some wood. Then he hired a little barrow and opened a timber yard.

German shopkeepers, even though they were naturalized, knew that they were likely to be in trouble after every air raid. The next morning an angry crowd, usually of women and children, might congregate outside their shop, hurling abuse and stones and looting goods through the broken windows.

There were similar anti-German riots after

21 The Cunard liner *Lusitania* was torpedoed by a German submarine and sunk off the Old Head of Kinsale, Ireland, on 7 May 1915. There were 2160 people on board and nearly 1500 men, women and children were drowned. The sinking of neutral ships was one factor which made the Americans enter the war in 1917.

any "atrocity", like the sinking of the *Lusitania* in 1915. At Gravesend, soldiers were sent in to disperse a mob of dockers who were wrecking and looting the premises of German shopkeepers. The entire stock of one furniture shop was pitched into the river.

It got so bad that many Germans adopted English surnames, including the Royal family who are of German origin. King George V, a cousin of the Austrian Kaiser, changed his name to Windsor in 1917.

5 Messengers of Death

Five hundred times as many soldiers were wounded *each day*, on average, as the total number of civilians injured during the *whole war*. One of the most vivid memories of wartime children was the sight of the blind, the crippled, the lame, stumbling along the streets in their hospital uniforms of "blue flannel suits and red ties".

Children remember seeing fleets of ambulances waiting outside railway stations to take the wounded off to large houses which had been converted into auxiliary hospitals for the duration of the war. The city of Chester alone received 160 special ambulance trains packed with injured soldiers.

Older girls helped to entertain the wounded. Mary Taylor (born 1898) says:

> My friend and I took out blind soldiers from St. Dunstan's – then in Regent's park. They liked the Variety at the Palladium on Saturday afternoons and we went to their dances.

Mabel Bell (born 1900) met her future husband, Herbert Bell (born 1897) when he returned to England, wounded.

> I first met Berty in his hospital blue at Bere Ferris. He brought a friend, Benny, who had also been wounded. We met them through the church. They came up to a little cottage my parents rented for about £10 a year as often as they could. We gave them strawberry and cream teas and had a sing-song after supper.

Mourning clothes
Another unforgettable wartime memory was

22   Mulgrave Castle in December 1914. In the first few weeks of the war, large houses and stately homes were taken over as hospitals for the wounded or used as convalescent homes. Many young VAD and Red Cross nurses also went to France to work in the front line hospitals.

the public display of grief for the fallen. After every big battle, the streets were full of children wearing black armbands or black ties, and women in mourning. Many families had to go into mourning more than once. Ernie Hancox (born 1900):

I had two brothers in the war, one in transport and the other in the infantry. One was killed in the Dardanelles. He was reported missing. We never knew what happened to him. The other one was reported missing in France.

Telegraph boys
Telegraph boys, who had the unpleasant task of delivering the news, became one of the most dreaded sights in every street. Mabel Bell (born 1900):

I can remember my mother going pale one afternoon as she saw a telegram boy coming towards the house. She turned to me and smiled as he cycled past, but she didn't say a word. My father and brother were in the Navy and you never knew if the telegram might be for you.

The telegrams stated baldly: "Regret to inform you that . . . was killed in action on . . . . Lord Kitchener sends his sympathy." After Kitchener's death in 1916, the Army Council expressed its sympathy instead.

Towards the end of the war, memorials to the dead began to be erected all over Britain. Rose Greaves (born 1908), whose father was the Vicar of the mill town of Morley, remembers:

My father was visiting families of men who had been killed all the time and he used to take me with him. We must have lost 100 young men. At the end of the war, marble tablets were put up in the church, all along one wall. There were so many of them.

23 **The telegraph boy was never a welcome visitor during the war.**

Churches all over Britain had temporary rolls of honour in their porches and some put up more permanent memorials. In the church of St Silas the Martyr in Kentish Town, London, for example, a shrine to the memory of "those fallen in battle belonging to the 1st Cadet Battalion, the Royal Fusiliers" was dedicated on 18 March, 1917.

In Chester Town Hall, on 23 May, 1918, the Bishop of Chester unveiled the city's provisional roll of honour while buglers sounded the Last Post.

The Cenotaph in Whitehall, which was designed by Sir Edwin Lutyens, was originally made of wood and put up temporarily for the peace celebrations on 19 July, 1919. It bears a simple inscription: "To Our Glorious Dead". Boys used to take off their caps and men used to doff their hats as a mark of respect whenever they passed it.

6 Children and the War Effort

Children helped the war effort in many ways. they raised hundreds of thousands of pounds for war charities by putting on entertainments in school and church halls, giving generously from their own pocket money to the numerous flag days and collecting salvage of all kinds: waste paper, bottles, rags and scrap metal. They also helped the men in the trenches and prisoners of war directly by sending them newspapers to read and food parcels.

Knitting parties
Girls – and their mothers – knitted endless socks, balaclava helmets and jumpers. Their enthusiasm sometimes ran away with them so much that their jumpers would have covered the average-sized soldier from head to foot.

Esme Strachey (born 1902) remembers:

> My mother organised "dog's wool" collecting at a depot and knitted it up. She got an MBE for that.

When Alice Hancox (born 1897) left school, she went to work in a factory in Kidderminster. When the war started it switched over from making carpets to knitting gloves and body warmers for soldiers. At night when she went home she would start knitting again to send to soldiers on the Western Front whom she had met at dances.

Rose Greaves (born 1908) recalls how the church, where her father was the vicar:

> had a working party to knit balaclava helmets and gloves. The women knitted them all through the war. The children

were set to make sandbags. We must have made hundreds of them.

Allotments
Later in the war, when food started to become scarce, children helped out the family rations by growing vegetables on allotments. By the end of the war there were nearly 1½ million allotments.

Boy Scouts and Girl Guides
The most highly organized war effort was made by the Boy Scouts. They had been formed in 1908 by Major General Robert Baden-Powell, the Boer War hero, who had stubbornly defended the little garrison town of Mafeking for 217 days until it was relieved by British forces. The Girl Guides were started by his sister in 1909.

Aims
The aims of the movement were to develop moral and physical cleanliness, character and initiative, by doing good turns, being thrifty, and learning how to survive in the open country by camping and scouting skills. The main emphasis was on patriotism: the need to show the rest of the world that British youth was ready to defend its country. In his handbook, *Scouting for Boys*, Baden-Powell wrote:

> Every boy should prepare himself by learning how to shoot and drill, to take his share in the defence of the Empire, if it should be attacked.

Girl Guides were also urged to "be prepared" in the event of an invasion.

Scouts in wartime

In 1914, there were nearly 150,000 Boy Scouts. They helped to bring in the harvests, served in soup kitchens and first-aid stations and cycled from one government department to another carrying messages. But their most highly publicized work was defending the country against "the enemy within our gates".

Spy mania

Only about a dozen spies were executed in Britain during the war, but people were

24 Boys Scouts undertook many of the jobs usually done by men. These boys are military despatch riders who carried messages from one army barracks to another. ▶

25 One of the jobs performed by Boy Scouts was to collect waste paper. The money raised from these collections was then spent on facilities for the wounded soldiers. This bath chair was presented to an Exeter hospital for the use of wounded soldiers who were convalescing there.

convinced there were thousands more who remained uncaptured.

At the outbreak of war, the whole country was swept by absurd rumours about German maids with caches of guns in their suitcases, spies shinning up telegraph poles to cut the wires and disrupt vital communications, and enemy agents driving furiously from one strategic point in the country to another, stopping only to change their number plates on the way. The rumours intensified when air raids began.

After the first Zeppelin attack on Norfolk in 1915, it was said that a motor-car had been seen on the esplanade at Wells-on-Sea with its lights pointing out to sea, to guide the airship to its target. A schoolmistress testified that she had heard the occupants of the car shout up to the Zeppelin, though it turned out later that the shouts had come from an equally suspicious, retired coastguard officer who had been trying to stop the car. Rumours of this kind never abated. Throughout the war, someone, somewhere, was always reporting flashing lights, mysterious motor-cars, or signals from windmills.

Scouts guard bridges

To save army manpower, the Scouts were given the task of guarding railway bridges throughout the country. One or two stood guard at the bridge itself to report any suspicious men to the police or the Territorials, while two other members of their patrol guarded the approaches to stop oncoming trains with flags. They camped near the bridge or slept in bivouac shelters, consisting of a piece of canvas thrown over a hurdle which was propped up by stakes driven into the ground.

The Scouts also guarded telegraph poles and reservoirs and were given special log books in

26 Girl Guides teaching refugee children English.

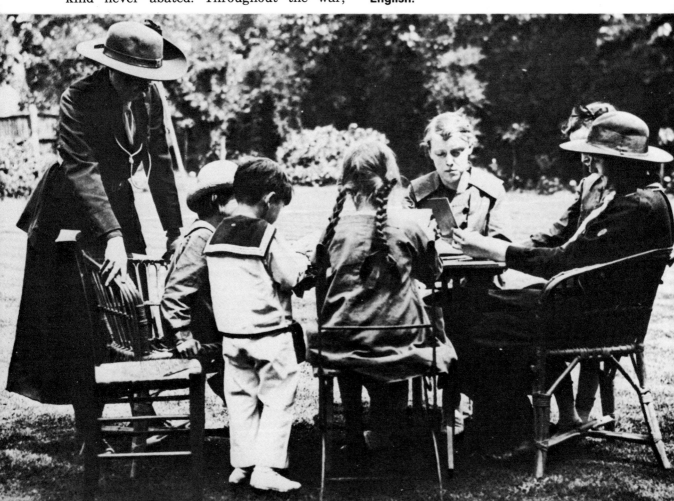

which they noted the numbers of suspicious cars. The Sea Scouts took over some duties from the coastguards.

Guides' work
Girl Guides did their good deeds by knitting socks and gloves for soldiers, caring for old ladies, and looking after Belgian refugees' children and trying to teach them English.

Belgian refugees

There was enormous sympathy at first for the refugees who flooded into England after "brave little Belgium" was invaded by the Germans at the beginning of the war. Well-meaning ladies who had gathered at Folkestone docks to welcome them with cups of tea, quite expected to find many children with their hands cut off. There were also other false reports about German atrocities, including one story that a priest had been tied to his church bell and used as a live clapper, that young children had been raped, and that the breasts of Belgian nuns had been cut off. Although the Germans had massacred 40 civilians in Aerschot and another 50 around Louvain, where they also burnt down the University library, the stories of their more lurid "atrocities" proved to be false.

About 100,000 Belgian refugees fled to Britain. Huge camps were set up for them at Earls Court and Edmonton in London, and 2500 local reception committees were established all over the country to find billets for them.

Public-spirited ladies opened up their homes, but very often the refugees were very different from what they had expected: sullen-looking peasants with care-worn wives and six or eight vacant-looking children, from whom they refused to be parted. Esme Strachey (born 1902) recalls:

> We heard about the atrocities in Belgium all the time. All Germans were suspect. The British also hated the Belgians who were considered sluttish as a consequence of the billeting.

There were just as many horror stories about Belgian refugees in the First World War as there were about child evacuees from cities in the Second World War, who were said to have infected their new homes with lice and fleas almost as soon as they arrived.

Not all of the refugees were as dirty, drunken or dissolute as rumour would have it. Many of them worked in munitions factories and integrated into the community. But it was never a very happy match. In some parts of the country, Belgians set up their own townships, several of which they named Elisabethville, after their popular queen, each with its own school, policemen and munitions factory. There was one at Birtley, Durham. Other families returned, disillusioned, to the small corner of their country which remained unoccupied, while some young men, when they came of age, also returned there to fight, and often die, in the trenches.

Enemy refugees
Meanwhile, on the other side of the fighting line, millions of displaced persons were undergoing much worse privations. After her terrifying enounter with the Cossacks in the woods, Zara Hershman (born 1910) finally reached her grandmother's flat in Vienna, where there was practically nothing to eat. Eventually, after visiting Budapest with her grandmother for three months, she rejoined her mother and the other children in Bohemia.

> My mother and the four children were living with other refugees in a school house in a little village. There was one enormous cooking range, heated by logs. My mother was very shy and could not fight to get at the oven, but sat in a corner with the little ones.

In 1917, they all returned to their home town.

> All the shops and businesses had been destroyed. There were very few houses left. Ours had gone, including the wonderful garden where my father had put up huge coloured balls on poles – like Belisha beacons – between the various flower beds.

7 Schools and Universities

When war was declared the education of some children was suddenly interrupted. Ann Vincent (born 1907):

> I remember I was in a primary school in Plymouth and it was taken over by Service people.

Many other children in other parts of the country arrived at school to find an armed sentry at the gate instead of the headmaster.

Most of the schools which had been used to house the thousands of men who had rushed to join "the colours" (regimental banners) were soon handed back; but education continued to be affected by the war in many other ways. Schools in some parts of London continued to close for part of the day throughout the war, because of fear of air raids and staff shortages.

The school system

In 1914, the educational system was rather different from today. The school-leaving age was only 12, though local authorities could raise it to 14 if they wished. But many did not do so, and those who did often granted so many exemptions that two out of five children still went out to work before the age of 14.

Elementary schools

The methods of education then were also rather different to schools today. In elementary schools the children sat in pairs on

28 This sentry is on guard at a school in London. The school was taken over the day the war started, obviously to the astonishment of these small children. The school became the barracks and sleeping accommodation for the men.

◄ 29 At the beginning of the war so many men volunteered that there was nowhere to house them, so many schools and other buildings were taken over. Later, large houses and church halls were used and the children returned to school. Notice the rifles still on the wall.

hard benches attached to wooden desks, with 50 or even more children in each class.

The schools concentrated on "the three Rs" – reading, writing and arithmetic – but there was also a smattering of other subjects such as history, geography, botany, art. Much of the learning was done by rote: the dates of all the English kings and queens and chunks of the New Testament (scripture was an important subject in elementary schools). Children who were considered to be not very bright were given sand and plasticine to play with instead. The girls were expected to wear white aprons and the boys starched collars, which they did

not remove when they did their "physical jerks" in the school play-ground.

Discipline was very strict. Children were not allowed to speak in class unless they had been asked a question by the teacher – and they were never allowed to leave their seat. In some schools they had to sit with their hands behind their backs when they were not writing. As in all schools at the time, canes, straps and rulers were used a lot. Rose Greaves (born 1908) remembers:

> I was at a little prep. school when the war started. I didn't like that school very much. I was always getting my knuckles rapped with a ruler.

Parents who were too poor to provide their children with boots kept them away from

30 A typical board school classroom. Boys and girls were taught separately, usually in different schools. When not actually writing, they had to sit with their arms folded or behind their backs. They wrote on slates with chalk.

school until they got a visit from the School Attendance Officer.

31 Children in a London school making articles of clothing for the war.

Wartime changes

By today's standards, schools were very poorly furnished and equipped, and rapidly rising prices during the war forced many of them to economize even further on books, paper and other essential materials. The size of classes increased in some schools as many teachers had volunteered to fight and they could not always be immediately replaced by women.

In some counties a great emphasis was placed on the righteousness of Britain's cause in history lessons, which dwelt at length on the nobility of recent heroes and heroines. Heroes like Jack Cornwell, the 17-year-old gunner on the *Chester* who remained at his post during the battle of Jutland though mortally wounded, for which he was postumously awarded the VC; and heroines like Edith Cavell, a British nurse in occupied Belgium, executed by the Germans in 1915 for helping Allied wounded to escape to neutral Holland.

Raising money for war charities, knitting and sewing, collecting waste materials and food for hospitals took up an increasing amount of children's time. Some authorities who raised the school-leaving age to 14 became more willing to let children leave school earlier, particularly in farming and industrial areas. There was also a great increase in the part-time employment of younger children outside school hours.

Secondary schools

Secondary education was provided at old-established grammar schools and new secondary schools, which had been set up by some local authorities after the 1902 Education Act. They all charged fees, though these were not as high as those charged by the independent public schools and private schools. But most of these secondary schools provided "free places" for a quarter of the pupils, which allowed a few brighter boys and girls from poorer homes to benefit from secondary education. Nevertheless, at the beginning of the war, only one in eight children was receiving any education after the age of 14.

Changes in secondary schools

Very few secondary schools were co-educational at that time. Although the pupils still spent much time on academic work, the war effort claimed a considerable amount of their spare time or intruded into lessons. Girls' secondary schools spent hours on entertainments, bazaars, knitting, sewing, collecting for hospitals and raising money for the men in the trenches and prisoners-of-war. Boys' schools either formed cadet corps or expanded the already existing O.T.C.

The trend that had begun before the war for an increasing number of children to go to secondary schools was not halted by the war. The total rose from 180,500 in 1914 to 216,500 in 1917. At the outbreak of war, many teachers in boys' schools had joined up voluntarily and had been replaced by women, who were by no means uniformly popular with the pupils.

Sidney Offord (born 1908), who had entered a kindergarten at four, then went to a Council school, where they tied his left hand behind his back to make him write with his right hand. He was sent to the old-established Grocers' Company's School in London when he was nine. It had 1200 boys, with 32 boys in each class.

We had women teachers at the school, but as soon as the war was over, they left. We didn't really like them.

You were graded according to ability. When I was in Form 2 I was 10, but some of the other boys were 14 or 15. One boy was an orphan. He was a dunce, but he was good at football and became an international player. He played for Tottenham.

We used to throw blotting paper on the ceiling. One of the boys had managed to lodge a pen nib in his blotting paper right above the teacher's desk. It fell down the bodice of her dress. She kept us in for that. But it served her right. She had a cheek to come in such a low-necked dress.

The Grocers' School was very good. If you went there, you were somebody. There was also a Central school, which was one grade above the normal Council schools.

Independent schools

Children of rich families either had a governess or tutor to teach them at home or went, usually as boarders, to one of the old, established public schools or one of the newer private ones.

The war had just as big an impact on their education.

Esme Strachey (born 1902) remembers her boarding schools where:

there was not enough food and we fought for the largest slice of bread and marge. When I left, I couldn't go to a finishing school in Europe, so I went to an evacuated school in Sunningdale instead, to learn French.

Public schools

Public schools then were very different from what they are today. They now tend to concentrate on academic ability, but in 1914 the main emphasis was on a sense of duty to King and country, sport and on producing gentlemen who would be able to run the Empire. Their OTCs provided the main strength of the officer class.

The Great War gave Old Boys from public schools the perfect opportunity to prove the value of their education and their courage. They did not fail, as their rolls of honour testify. Of the 5650 Old Etonians who went on active service, 1157 were killed and 1467 were wounded. They were awarded 1999 honours, including 13 V.C.s, 584 D.S.O.s and 744 M.C.s. Of the 2225 former pupils of Tonbridge School who saw active service, 1625 were commissioned. There were 415 killed, 508

32 These little girls, in their neat, well-made dresses, came from well-off families. Before the war, there would normally have been a headmaster and male teachers. These were gradually replaced by women as the men went off to fight.

wounded, and 692 war honours were awarded, including one V.C.

As these Old Boys gazed across the desolate wastes of no-man's-land their thoughts sometimes reverted, particularly on Sundays, to their school and its creed and the chapel which had given them the faith to face the enemy. As Sag Harvey wrote in 1915 in the *Portcullis*, the magazine of Emanuel School, Wandsworth Common:

Dear old Emanuel, what a treasure house of happy memories! It is all so easy to picture – the mellow light, the choir, the old familiar faces in the old familiar pews and S. . ., good old S. . ., tucked away in his corner, ready to lower the lights when the sermon begins.

Thus one dreams, but the crackle of the machine-guns brings one back to earth, to remember that this is war, that just over there is the Hun and that between us is about fifty yards of good French soil.

Sag Harvey and 93 other Old Boys from Emanuel School were to die in the war.

Universities

Like public schools, universities were mainly the preserve of the rich, until state scholarships, which were introduced after the First World War, allowed a few more exceptionally gifted children from poorer homes to attend them.

Almost as soon as war broke out, the quadrangles of colleges at Oxford and Cambridge were deserted apart from foreign undergraduates and the unfit. Some of the colleges later provided accommodation for officer cadets. Many of the undergraduates and graduates were killed, including Raymond Asquith, the son of the Prime Minister, Rupert Brooke, the poet and William Gladstone, a grandson of the former Liberal Prime Minister.

8 Clothes

At the beginning of the war, clothes were still very similar to the styles worn in the Edwardian era. There were no special styles for children's clothes; they were dressed like miniature adults. All children wore many more clothes than they do today and, even in the summer, were covered in several layers.

Girls' clothes

Girls during this period wore a vest, a camisole (a kind of sleeveless blouse) made of calico, stays (a kind of fleecy-lined, sleeveless jacket, buttoned up the front) and full-length petticoats. The white petticoats were made of cotton, usually trimmed with lace. But there was a difference between the materials used for middle-class and working-class children's clothes. Better-off children might have satin or chiffon underskirts, or even black satin or Japanese silk. There might be a 12-inch pleated flounce at the bottom hem, trimmed with lace and ribbon. The camisole would be trimmed with lace and tied at the waist with ribbon. There was also a corset bodice for children of all ages, made of cotton or cambric, and this was boned and shaped to the figure. These were even made for infants in 20-inch chest sizes – for three- or four-year-olds!

In the winter, combinations (combs, as they were called) were added to the undergarments. These were similar to modern culottes with wide legs and were embroidered with lace and frills. They were made of Nainsook, a thick sort of Indian muslin, rather like the cheap Indian dresses and blouses on sale today.

Rose Greaves (born 1908) remembers:

I had black stockings and laced-up boots. My mother said I had to wear boots, then I would have nice ankles. I wore combinations and a liberty bodice with suspenders buttoned on. Also a sort of bodice called a Hug-me-tight. Then on top a flannelette petticoat. But I was always cold.

Knickers, made of jersey or flannel, reached to the knees. They were usually black or navy blue. There were complete outfits of nightdress, combs, knickers, camisole and stays.

To keep up the long, black, woollen stockings worn by all girls there were elastic suspenders attached to a belt which went round the hips. Babies were covered in layers of frilly petticoats, trimmed with lace. They had rubber pants over their nappies which must have been very hot and uncomfortable. Once out of nappies they wore frilly white knickers, but these were changed at an early age to blue or black. Their dresses were long-sleeved and were made of white muslin or silk, with layers of lace and frills. Appearance was all that mattered for babies' and children's clothes. Children had to look pretty and comfort was not considered important. Little girls at the seaside might be allowed to tuck their dresses into their knickers when they were paddling and, by 1914, even older girls began to do this, but most clothes were for show.

Girls' outer garments were also quite restrictive. Sailor suits were popular for younger girls, with collars trimmed with white cord and pleated skirts in navy-blue

33 Skirts were still long during the war and even girls working in factories continued to wear long, full skirts with an overall on top. Only girls working on the land were bold enough to wear slacks. Most children and young girls had long hair which was tied back in a bun as they got older.

serge. Many of the collars were detachable, which would have been popular with the less well-off because they could be transferred from one dress to another. By 14, girls went into long skirts and wore styles similar to their mothers.

Smock dresses were popular with all classes and were made of muslin, cotton or silk, according to your class. These dresses were pleated at the front and the back. This made them attractive to the poorer people because they could let out the pleats as the child grew.

Skirts were full in 1916, but became straighter by the end of the war. Gym tunics emerged at the beginning of the war. They were not worn in elementary schools but were gradually adopted in secondary schools. They were later also worn in private schools, but the early ones look very different from the gym slips we know today. They were still long dresses and had very deep box pleats; if a blouse was worn underneath only the collar, and the sleeves would show.

The Girl Guides' regulation dress was a long, navy, jersey dress, tie, dark blue stockings, a straw hat and a cape. A dress similar to this was worn at many girls' schools.

All girls wore a hat out-of-doors, the most popular types being sailor hats and flat straw hats, or straw hats with a round brim. But rich children might, for best, wear a wide-brimmed hat with flowers, just like their mothers'. Their long hair was tied back with ribbons and, if parted, the parting was usually in the centre. Nice little girls also wore gloves made of kid.

Coats were made of wool, cashmere or serge and many girls had a muff made of imitation fur. They wore woollen socks under long, buttoned or laced, black boots. Older girls from richer families would also own a pair of buckle shoes for best.

Working-class children always wore a starched, white, muslin pinafore, which

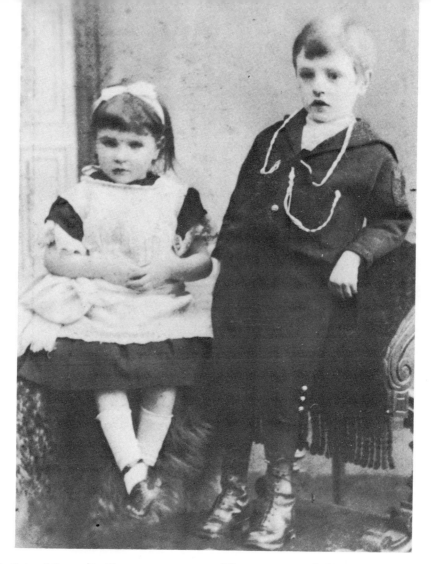

34 Typical clothes of the period for poorer children. The little boy is wearing a simple version of the sailor jacket. The little girl wears the pinafore smock worn by all working-class children.

usually had a frill around it. This gradually developed into a frock pinafore with a sash and could be made of holland (hard-wearing linen fabric), cotton or wool. Rose Greaves (born 1908):

My two cousins wore longer clothes than I did. I thought they were rather old-fashioned, and they always wore starched white pinafores.

Many poorer children wore a white pinafore all the time, even to school.

Wartime changes
During the war, women's clothes gradually changed and, as children's clothes were simply smaller versions of the adults', they changed too. Women working in munitions factories and on the land could not have frills and flounces. They began to wear a kind of long frock coat, which was adopted by women from all walks of life. Only the materials varied, according to class and occupation. Girls' clothes became looser, with wider pleated skirts and might be made of cotton, silk or wool.

40

Children's long hair was still tied back with ribbons, although long ringlets were still popular for special occasions, such as having a photograph taken. Women in factories and those working on the land gradually changed to shorter, bobbed hair and gradually, although not until the end of the war, it became acceptable for older girls to have shorter hair, lightly waved with curling tongs.

During the war, many women were in mourning and so dressed all in black but clothes in general became brighter. Navy blue or black stockings were replaced by white and cream and black or white or pastel dresses by more daring colours. Young girls wore three-quarter length socks instead of the long wool stockings. The corset bodice became less common and finally disappeared, and there were fewer petticoats. Celanese was replacing the stiffer materials used previously. Skirts on coats and dresses had become about two inches shorter, although it was not until the 1920s that they became really short.

Clothes for special occasions
During the war, there were fewer parties and special occasions but white weddings continued. In October 1917 one newspaper report of a wedding in London stated that the six bridesmaids wore:

> gowns of shot blue and silver silk with ninon overdresses and wreaths of red leaves. They carried sheaves of crysanthemums tied with tulle and sprays of heather.

At another wedding, in April 1918:

> the three bridesmaids wore pale blue crepe de Chine and black velvet hats with roses.

Boys' clothes
Like the girls, boys did not have special styles but were dressed like little men. In fact, the aim was for their clothes to look "manly". Even three-year-olds wore navy-blue serge or tweed sailor suits with a belted jacket and for small

35   A white wedding. This bride still wears the traditional white wedding dress and carries a bouquet of flowers. Most group wedding photos were taken in the backyard or garden because ordinary people would have the reception at home rather than in a hall or hotel.

36 This wedding reflects a more sombre situation. This bride's first husband was killed in the trenches by a mustard gas attack. There are no bouquets and most of the ladies are in dark clothes. Many widows re-married during the war. Often they had been married for only a few weeks or months when their husbands went to France and they never saw them again.

boys there were also tartan suits with sailor hats. Older boys wore the suit with long wide trousers and in the summer they had white drill trousers. Little boys' trousers reached to the knees.

The naval look, the popular sailor suit worn by both boys and girls, reflected the Royal Family's associations with the navy and people copied them, just as today people tend to copy the styles worn by the present Royal Family. Prince Edward, later to become Edward VIII, and his brothers were photographed in sailor suits and the rest of the population followed. It started off as a white summer suit for small boys, mainly for wearing at the sea-side but was then made in navy blue serge to wear in the winter. The trousers were bell-bottomed, like sailors' or there were knee-length knicker-bockers.

Throughout the war, apart from sailor suits, the most common style for boys was the straight Edwardian-type jacket and serge or tweed knicker-bockers. Boys of 14 upwards wore these.

Children from wealthier families also wore black or blue velvet suits or velvet jackets with navy blue trousers. And, in 1914, pleated Norfolk jackets with patch pockets and a tight belt were popular with middle-class boys and the flannel blazer had been introduced. This was worn by boys of all classes and became a part of school uniform, as it still is today.

Perhaps the most desirable outfit, although too expensive for many, was the Eton suit, a copy of that worn by the boys at Eton College.

This consisted of grey trousers, a black serge jacket which fitted tightly at the waist, with wide revers ending at the waist and a high-buttoned waistcoat. Boys who were actually at Eton during the war often wore short or long flannel trousers with a striped cap.

All boys' suits included a waistcoat with a high V-neck fastening. Shirts all had a narrow, stiff collar attached with studs and this was worn even by small boys. Ribbed stockings reaching above the knee were the normal thing, with boots laced or buttoned down the side, buttoned boots being mainly for younger boys. Children from wealthier families had patent leather boots which they might even wear on weekdays.

Only poor children went out without a hat. All other boys would wear a cloth cap, a sailor hat or a flat, straw hat and older boys from better-off families might have top hats for Sundays.

During the war, pyjamas came to replace the night-shirt of the Edwardian era.

By the end of the war, a version of the straight Edwardian jacket was still the most common style for most boys, with black trousers, black boots and a large cap which covered the head. Large families still favoured the smock dress for girls, because it could be let out and handed down till it was worn out.

Poor children

Poor children had very few clothes at all. They might be lucky enough to have discarded clothes given to them, otherwise, their mothers bought remnants and old clothes in the markets. Many children had no socks and some had to go to school with no boots. Often boys had only ragged shirts, with no jackets. The number of very poor did decrease during the war because, for the first time, many women had an income and there was an allowance from the army for the families of all serving soldiers. But what a child wore still reflected his or her social standing and the great divisions between rich and poor.

37 Boys' clothes were like a uniform because they were all so similar. The straight Edwardian jacket was still worn, although it always looked rather shapeless. Many boys wore a kind of bloomer with long woollen socks like the two on the right of the picture. All but the very poorest boys wore caps.

9 Holidays and Entertainments

The variety of toys was as great in 1914 as it is today, but a child would not have expected to own the vast number of toys that many children have now.

The production of toys had been going on for over 100 years and, apart from the new technological toys and games, there are few toys today which could not have been bought in the First World War. Because plastic did not exist they were made in more durable materials than today and the designs were usually better.

Every child, except the very poorest, would have had a ball of some sort, usually made of rubber, and also a spinning top. For babies and little children there were pull toys, skittles and beautifully carved and painted hobby horses. There were wooden building bricks with coloured designs on all sides of the bricks to make into a picture, and there were shaped bricks for building into houses and farmyards. There were also many animals to go with the farmyard and rag dolls, golliwogs, teddy bears, squeaky toys and furry animals for babies were all available.

Girls' toys

All little girls would have had a doll; poor children might have a wooden, painted doll, which could be home-made but, for all but the very poor, there was an amazing variety of beautiful dolls. Some were made with rubber faces and cloth bodies. Some were made of celluloid. There were even tin and steel dolls with painted faces and hair. But the best dolls were made in Germany and had porcelain heads and leather bodies stuffed with sawdust. Their faces were delicately moulded and painted and they had long hair. They were jointed and could walk and move their arms and eyes. Although these German dolls disappeared from the shops during the war,

38 The collecting of tin soldiers greatly increased in popularity during the war years. Note the Red Cross cart, used to transport the wounded from the battlefield.

many of the dolls loved by children at that time would have been made in Germany. Thousands of them had been exported before the war and they were popular because they were cheaper than their French counterparts. The Germans also made sleeping baby dolls, and "character" dolls with crying faces. They were dressed in lovely clothes and toy shops sold a great range of dolls' accessories, shoes, hats and muffs as well as the equipment necessary for feeding them.

Little girls also had all the domestic toys necessary at that time, from toy mangles, buckets, mops and brushes to clothes-horses and washing tubs. With the tin ovens, which could be heated by a tiny candle to cook for the dolls' parties, went all the cutlery and crockery and even saucepans made of brass. Often the tiny china tea-sets were kept on the mantelpiece for safety.

Children's sewing machines were brightly painted with colourful designs. There were dolls' prams made in many styles in walnut, birch and wicker. Dolls' cots were often made of metal, like real beds, and dolls' rocking chairs were made of walnut. Toy shops were popular, too, with their long counters, scales and display stands. Tea, sugar and salt were kept in little drawers and had to be weighed out with a tiny scoop. The imitation fruit and vegetables were made of plaster. During the war, you could still get little packets of branded goods to sell in toy shops.

Boys' toys and games

For little boys, millions of tin-plate, metal iron and clockwork toys were produced. The tin models were called "penny toys", although they actually cost 2d or 3d, and included early aeroplanes, vans, balloons, and fire-engines and, during the war, tiny Zeppelins. Many of these toys were mechanical and a large range of tin aircraft was made. Toy cars were generally larger and better made than those of today; there was even one model made of ivory with a clockwork motor.

Trains were also popular with boys and they often had a track which went right round the room. Sidney Offord (born 1908) remembers:

> I had clock-work trains. We always had a biggish house. In those days, you had lino on upstairs floors with rugs. You only had carpets downstairs. At Christmas, I used to sleep on the top floor and the relatives could hear my train reverberating through the floor. Some of them used to give me 5/- for a Christmas present.

But probably the most desirable toy was the model soldier. These had been collected by boys for many years but their popularity increased, naturally, during the war.

They had previously been made in wood, tin, lead or papier mâché but William Britain had begun to make hollow figures, which were easier and cheaper to produce. By 1914, they were not only being sold in thousands in this country but were also being exported to Germany and other countries. These soldiers were accurate in every detail – their uniforms, shapes and colours – even down to the stripes. The horses' trappings also had to be the correct colour for their particular regiment or brigade.

A reduced production of model soldiers continued throughout the war. There were field guns, vehicles and mounted troops in colourful uniforms carrying their banners. There were howitzers and 13-pounder guns. You could buy a set of infantry or a military band with drums and flags. There were even wounded soldiers on horseback, with the horse standing, terrified, on its hind legs.

Some boys collected 400 or 500 soldiers and laid out their army in battle formation. There was no better present than to be given a "Box of Britains". Winston Churchill, as a boy, had 1500 such soldiers which he laid out in battle formation. It was this which made his father suggest that he should go into the army. One firm making these toys issued instructions on how to set out the battlefield, armies, troops, ammunition, casualties, and even prisoner-of-war camps.

39 A "Trick Pony" money box. Money is put in the horse's mouth, he rears up and deposits in the box.

Germany had also been a great producer of model soldiers and there were societies there and in other European countries, including Britain. They exchanged soldiers and information about the history of the regiment. But, during the war, the German model-soldier industry collapsed and the societies ceased to exist. However, they both continued on a limited scale throughout Britain. In 1919, the Treaty of Versailles prohibited the making of military emblems so no more could be produced.

There were other games, too. One, with toy soldiers, was called "Little Wars" and could be played with two, four or six players; it usually took one whole evening to complete a game.

There was "War Draughts" played with cardboard counters and "War Chess" where the chessmen were in the uniform of particular regiments. Other games included "North Sea Tactics", "Advance", "The Way to Constantinople", "Spy", "March on Berlin" and "The Silver Bullet" (where there was a silver ball which had to find its way "home" along a winding road to Berlin).

There were also toy guns, bows and arrows and wooden warships for boys to play with, and they could dress up in uniforms of various regiments. Model-making was popular and boys at a school in Surrey founded a model aero club in 1915. Boys also collected bits of aluminium from Zeppelin salvage to make into toys.

Children in the First World War were as keen on collecting as many children are today.

As well as shrapnel souveniers, cigarette cards were popular items to collect. Sidney Offord (born 1908):

> My grandmother used to let rooms. She had a large house. Flats weren't self-contained then. One of her tenants gave me boxes and boxes of cigarette cards, sets of them. Her son had gone away to the war. I wish I'd kept them.

Comics and books

Comics and weekly magazines were very popular. *The Magnet* and *The Gem*, were 2d each and you could get four *Sexton Blakes* a month for 4d each, telling stories of the well-known detective. Another one, called *The Boy's Friend*, was also 4d and contained school stories; Billy Bunter was the best-known character. For girls, there was the *Girl's Own Paper*.

There was, of course, a wide variety of

40 A typical sitting room of the First World War period. The doll's face would be made of porcelain, and the doll's clothes were very elaborate. Often children were only allowed to play with these precious dolls on Sundays.

children's books, many with a moral and religious tone. The stories tended to be sad and sentimental but the Annuals were full of more cheerful stories and poems. There were books telling little girls how they should treat their dolls and how they should teach them manners and good behaviour. This, of course, was really meant to apply to the little girls themselves.

Sunday toys

Many parents at that time still had very Victorian attitudes. They thought it was wrong to enjoy oneself too much on a Sunday and children were expected to sit in the parlour and to be seen and not heard. Better-off and middle-class children often had a nanny to look after them and she would keep a sharp eye on their behaviour.

Children were taught to take care of their toys and often were only allowed to play with them at specific times. Only certain toys were thought of as suitable to be played with on a Sunday and these were known as "Sunday toys". Card games and draughts would be disapproved of on a Sunday, but a child might play with a Noah's Ark, because that was religious, or read Bible stories, or even make a jigsaw – if it had a religious theme.

Outdoor toys

Outdoor toys included go-carts and pedal cars, and tricycles and scooters became popular with boys and girls after their invention in 1913. There were toy parachutes and kites to fly, garden tools, fishing rods, yoyos, stilts, swings and roundabouts. Most children had a hoop of some kind. Rose Greaves (born 1908):

I had a wooden hoop and a stick and I used to run round the park with it, along the footpaths. The boys had iron hoops with the stick attached, so they had to run very fast to keep up with it.

The supply of toys in the shops diminished during the war. The *Hampshire Telegraph and Post* reported on 28 December, 1917, that there were no toys in Handley's winter sale at Southsea.

Poor children

Poor children had very few toys – probably a drum, hoop, rag doll and paper dolls. Throughout the war, paper dolls could still be bought and they also appeared in women's magazines. These were cardboard cut-outs, complete with clothes in which they could be dressed. Paper children could also be cut from papers and magazines and arranged in rows, as though they were in a classroom. Children got endless pleasure from these simple cut-outs.

Newspapers and brown paper could also be used for paper-folding and made into such things as aeroplanes and tanks. For the rest, they made their own from boxes, bits of wood and anything they found in the road. If they had a ball, they would play football in the streets.

Football matches were discontinued eight months after the war started, after the Cup Final on 24 April 1915. (Rugby matches had been abandoned at the start of the war, but horse-racing continued throughout the war.) The Football Association gave a lot of money to war charities, and boys who went to those early wartime football matches used to listen to the recruiting speeches made at the end of the matches by well-known people. During the week, they could go to the football grounds and watch the new army recruits practising their drill. Soldiers continued to play football throughout the war in their regiments and boys continued to practise in the streets.

Children used to spend a lot of time hanging around corners in city or village streets, waiting for a car to go past or anything else entertaining to happen. (Very few children had ever been for a ride in a car in 1914, when there were only 200,000 motor vehicles of any kind on the roads.) They had even more time to stand and stare after Summer Time was introduced in 1916 and the clocks were put back one hour to save on fuel.

If they were lucky, they might be taken to a magic lantern show, which was free. These were usually shown at church and village halls and dealt with religious topics or the work of missionaries in darkest Africa.

Cinemas, music halls and variety shows

Cinema was popular with children in cities, although they were not very comfortable places. They were known as "fleapits" and children could get in for ½d.

All the films were silent, all were in black and white, and many were comedies. Children enjoyed Charlie Chaplin and Buster Keaton and also adventure films. Although there was no talking in the film, a pianist in the cinema

PROFESSOR LIKONTI'S
WONDERFUL ROUMANIAN
FLEA CIRCUS

MUST BE SEEN TO BE BELIEVED.

PATRONISED BY ROYALTY NOBILITY, AND CLERGY.

ome and see the IVELY FLEAS Dance a Ballet, ght a Duel with Swords, Walk the Tight ope a la Blondin

Harnessed like horses, and drawing and driving Hansom Cabs, Mail Vans, Funeral Cars, Cabriolets, Milk Cars Artillery Fleas firing a Cannon.

The SMALLEST PERFORMERS in the World Interesting alike to Old and Young, Rich, and Poor.

BEWARE OF THE DOG

played suitable music as an accompaniment.

From 1916 onwards, children saw more realistic films. War films were being made about the fighting on the Western Front. Official films of the Battle of the Somme were shown all over the country and boys and girls saw what war was really like.

There were also music hall and variety shows. There were no reserved seats and children queued outside to pay for their wooden plank seats in the gallery. There were musicals and, at Christmas, pantomimes. Mary Taylor (born 1898):

> Of course, the boys were always coming home on leave from France and loved the musicals – *The Maid of the Mountains, Revue A to Z, Lilac Domino, Chu Chin Chow* – so we had many trips there.

Songs from variety shows and musicals were equally popular with children. There were no transistors – not even radios – in those days, so children on their way to school and errand

41   When the fair came to town it was a time of great excitement and the flea circus would always attract a large crowd.

42   Young factory girls giving a special performance for soldiers. Many firms, munitions workers and school-children organized entertainments for the troops.

boys whistled in the streets. The songs they whistled and sang were the ones which happened to be most popular at the time.

1914 "Keep the Home Fires Burning"
     "Sister Susie's Sewing Shirts"
     "Under the Bridges of Paris"
1915 "Pack Up Your Troubles"
1916 "If You were the Only Girl in the World"
     "Roses of Picardy"
     "Take Me Back to Dear Old Blighty"
1917 "Good-Bye-Ee"
     "Over There"
1918 "Rock-a-Bye Your Baby with a Dixie Melody"

Holidays and outings

Most children did not have a seaside holiday in the summer, though many of them had day excursions for Whit Monday or August Bank Holiday.

Almost all children went to Sunday School and every year there would be an outing. At some Sunday schools there were 150-200 children and they used to go in charabancs (motor coaches) to a nearby seaside town or into the country. There would be games and races and, for tea, sandwiches, cakes and lemonade.

Another popular day out was the annual summer pub outing. Most of the local pubs

organized these and it was usually only for the men. The children used to go along to see them off and to greet them when they returned.

Many children stayed with relatives for their holidays. Rose Greaves (born 1908):

> We had no holidays during the war, not until 1919. We used to go to Brighton to see relatives. We took the tram to Leeds and the train to Kings Cross and then to Brighton. My father used to take me to the front of the train to look at the engine, to see the coal being stoked up on the fire.

Some people stayed in lodgings; more prosperous families stayed in a boarding house and some rented a whole house, with the

44 Life at the seaside. During the war, girls took the place of the nursemaids and mothers who had gone into war work.

landlady living in the basement. Hotels and villas were reserved for the rich. Sidney Offord (born 1908) remembers:

> When war was declared, we were going on the East coast, but Father cancelled it. There were German cruisers there and they shelled Felixstowe. I remember quite a lot of people were killed in Great Yarmouth.
>
> We went to Worthing in 1916. There was no booking in those days. They left me on the front with the suitcases and they eventually found accommodation at 9 o'clock. We went there for three summers.

Seaside resorts had been at the height of their popularity as holiday centres when the war began, and year after year people who could afford holidays used to return to the same place for their holidays. For those children who lived near the sea, there was always

◄ **43 In spite of the war, people still went to the seaside on both sides of the Channel and it was even possible for French people to come to England if they were willing to risk the German submarines. Here an English soldier is playing with French children on the beach.**

entertainment. Pierrot clowns were still entertaining at Brighton during the war.

On some beaches, there was still segregration of the sexes, but girls and boys now wore a one-piece swimming suit which came down almost to their knees and the old bathing machines of the Victorian era were used merely as changing huts. Many children were not allowed to bathe, but only to paddle. Children always had their photos taken by the "resident" photographer who spent the summer parading up and down the beach. There was little sun-bathing, because very little of the body was actually exposed and a tanned skin was not considered fashionable then.

The most exciting thing at the seaside was the pier, made of iron, with its pavilion and minarets and domes. On the pier, children could see performing fleas, have their fortune told, watch people in flames diving into the sea, listen to the bands, have tea, peep through the 1d slot machines at gruesome scenes or laugh at "what the butler saw". There were cheap china souveniers, gaudy postcards and pull-out cards with views.

Mabel Bell (born 1900) recalls:

We loved the pier. As a kid I loved to fish and sometimes caught a small plaice or eels and we had concerts frequently. You could go on the pier for about 1d or 2d. They had lots of slot machines and you could get cigarettes for very little and bars of chocolate.

Some parents continued to take their children abroad for their holidays as it was still easy to cross the Channel. Throughout the war, there were advertisements in newspapers enticing rich people to go and stay on the French Riviera, though probably few people took advantage of these offers. And other young people came the other way – to England – to work. Raymonde Butcher (born 1899) explains:

In 1917, I was a children's governess in Paris. The family decided to come to England and they brought me with them. I came on a ferry from Le Havre to Southampton. I stayed in the village of Heswell. Then I lived in Liverpool. There was plenty of food in the market. It was full of good things like lobster. We used to go to the market every week.

10 Wartime Work

In the first few months of the war, employers reduced their work forces owing to business uncertainties and many young people could not get a job. Juvenile Employment Exchanges, which had been set up in 1910 to cope with persistent pre-war unemployment, were crowded with young school-leavers of 14 looking for work.

Things were so bad in London that they were advised to go back to school. Special classes were held for unemployed school-leavers (the forerunners of the YTS) and recreation clubs and workrooms were established. But, by December 1914, with so many men going to fight, the situation had completely changed. There were more jobs for boys than applicants and the labour shortage went on in some occupations until 1918. Employment of young people went up by 18 per cent between 1914 and 1917. Wars always help to cut the dole queues.

The demand for labour became so great that many local authorities allowed boys to leave school early. It was estimated that over a third of boys in Sheffield and half in Leeds left school when they were just over 13. When they left school, some young lads, like Ernie Hancox (born 1900), took the first job they were offered.

I was a chauffeur. I left school when I was 14, the first year of the war. The previous chauffeur had gone into the army and I took his place. Of course, I'd never driven a car before but I got in and picked it up as I went along.

There was no driving test in those days and no insurance, though petrol was rationed. You were only allowed to use it for important purposes.

The man I worked for was an inspector of horses. He used to select the ones that were to go to the front. Later I drove a 1916 Ford.

Although many boys took the nearest job when they left school, others seized the opportunities that the war provided for much better-paid employment.

Changes in boys' employment

There were big changes in the kind of work boys did during the war. Many school-leavers who would have worked on the land or have become clerks, or joined the Post Office as telegraph boys now went to work for much higher wages in munitions factories, chemical plants or in transport.

A boy of 13 or 14 could earn £2 a week working in a munitions factory compared with the 10/- (50p) a week of a farm lad. For this the munitions worker had to work extremely long hours – 60 hours a week was the permitted maximum, though some unscrupulous employers often made employees exceed this. They often had to work on Sundays and at night. In those days, however, everybody worked longer hours. Farm lads, for example, worked from 7 a.m. to 5 p.m. and were often out in the fields in the coldest weather, hedging and ditching, their shoulders protected from the freezing wind by a piece of old sacking.

Changes in girls' employment

Many more girls went out to work during the

war, instead of staying at home to help their own mother or going out to help someone else's by becoming a domestic servant. At the beginning of the war, 300,000 girls under 18 were "in service", which was the main occupation for girls from poorer homes. A few worked in big houses but far more often they were ill-paid, badly treated skivvies in houses which were sometimes not much grander than their own.

Domestic service was already unpopular with most girls and the war gave them an opportunity to escape, leaving their employers speechless with indignation. There were complaints in many newspapers and magazines about the difficulties of running houses without servants and the indignities of having to do the cooking and the cleaning for oneself. The normal middle-class home had three servants: a cook, a parlour-maid and a nursery-maid. The newspapers had pages full of advertisements for servants: "a respectable soldier's widow would suit", or "an experienced parlour-maid – £24 a year".

Some girls took over jobs which were done almost exclusively by boys in pre-war days, becoming messengers, errand girls for shopkeepers and tradesmen and telegraph girls. (During the war, the number of boys employed by the Post Office fell by nearly 7000 and the number of girls increased by nearly 4000.) They also took over jobs which would formerly have been done by boys in building, wood-working, mines and quarries, and in many other occupations.

Factory work
A much larger number of girls went to work in factories. Some took up traditional female jobs, becoming machinists, finishers, and pressers, in clothing factories which had switched over from producing civilian clothes to uniforms for the Forces. But most of them went to work in munitions factories where the rates of pay were much higher.

In all factories, the girls' conditions and hours of work were more carefully regulated than the boys'. In 1916, girls under 16 were not allowed to work at night or to do overtime. In some factories, they were provided with free milk and, at Crosse and Blackwell's factory in Battersea, they were provided with a free dinner and free education as well, though they had to stay until 7 p.m. to receive it. They worked from 8 a.am. to 11.30 a.m., and then they had physical exercises for three-quarters of an hour, to give them a good appetite for the free dinner. They were back in the factory from 1.15 p.m. to 4 p.m. and after tea, which only cost 1d, they had lessons from 5 p.m. to 7 p.m., just as if they were back at school again.

Office work
The biggest increase, however, was in the employment of girls in offices, insurance companies, City institutions and banks, to do work which had previously been done by men. Mary Taylor (born 1898):

I was 16 when the war started and was on a commercial course at Clark's College in London. In March 1915 I got a job in the

45 These girls are working in an aeroplane factory, covering an axle fairing with fabric. As the years passed, women and girls took over more and more complicated work and some became mechanics and engineers. But after the war these jobs were all given back to men.

City. My days were full, as we worked from 9.30 a.m. to 5.30 p.m. and till 1 p.m. on Saturdays.

It was the beginning of the end of the male clerk, about half a million of whom had volunteered or been conscripted. When they came back from the trenches, they found a very different world and women were never dislodged from offices as they were from many other places of wartime employment.

Part-time work

In 1914 it was estimated that a quarter of a million school children did some part-time work, and the number increased greatly during the war. Some of the children did this work in school-time. In agricultural areas, some boys of 11 and over were given exemptions to work every morning or afternoon on a farm and, in some textile areas, girls of 12 and over could be exempted to work in factories in the same way. But the majority of children did their part-time jobs before they went to school. In one London district, a boy of

46 Many college girls became agricultural workers, some even became trainers of the horses which were needed in France. Many took up nursing and ambulance work. These girls are having a drink at a pump after helping with the flax harvest.

eight got up at 6 a.m. every day to deliver papers. There were older boys, too, who worked a 25-hour week. Milk boys in the same area of London, whose ages ranged from eight to 13, started even earlier – at 4.30 a.m. – and worked until 6 a.m. Some other boys worked in coalyards.

There was a great demand for these part-time workers, as the boys who would normally have done many of these jobs full-time were now working in factories for much higher wages. Although the jobs were often very poorly paid, the families needed the extra money as, throughout the war, inflation sent prices soaring.

The ill-effect of these early-morning jobs on children's health and education was pointed out in one official report after another. A

55

memorandum issued by the Board of Education in 1918 said:

> War conditions have increased the demand for child labour. About 10% of the children in attendance in public elementary schools in the area investigated are employed out of school hours, often in most unsuitable work and for inadequate pay. The effects are detrimental to their progress in school.

In some towns, as much as 40 per cent of elementary school children had a part-time job, but little was done to stop it.

Mothers' work
Many mothers had a hard struggle to bring up the family. Ernie Hancox (born 1900):

> My father died when I was a few months old, so my mother supported us by doing washing and charring. There were eight of us, although two of my sisters died when they were young.
> My mother did the washing in a big tub. She had to walk three miles to work and three miles back again every day. She also did the scrubbing of the floors where she worked. They were great stone floors. That was how she made enough to keep us. There was nothing else. No other money.

Those families where the father was still alive but serving with the Forces were somewhat better off, as a mother with two children received an allowance of 21/- (£1.05p) a week. But this was insufficient to keep them. As a result, there was a great increase, (about 50 per cent) in the number of women working during the war. They not only worked in munitions factories but also did all kinds of jobs which had been vacated by men having to serve in the Forces – crane-driving, carpentry, concrete-mixing, driving horse-drawn delivery vans, sweeping chimneys, welding – though they were to lose their jobs when the men came back.

First crèches
To make life easier for mothers working in munitions factories, some crèches were opened. One of the first was opened in London by Sylvia Pankhurst, the suffragette, who took over an East-End public house, the Gunmakers' Arms, whose licence had been withdrawn, and turned it into the Mothers' Arms, with white-painted walls, bright chintz curtains and accommodation for 40 children.

War profiteers
Despite inflation, which reduced the value of the pound by about 60 per cent during the war, there were a number of people who prospered, such as families with several sons and daughters working in munitions factories. The owners of the factories usually benefitted much more, as did other profiteers in food, ship-building, horses and timber. Most of the eight million or more men who were still in civilian employment managed to keep their

47 Girl Guides looking after small children whose mothers are at work.

48   There was little provision for children of working mothers and so in most areas local women organized facilities such as nursery schools, playgrounds and crêches.

heads above water financially. There were far fewer goods to spend money on in any case, and much of the money went on necessities such as food. Drunkenness, which had been a problem early in the war, particularly among shipyard and munitions workers, was curbed when pubs were shut in the afternoons and customers were prohibited by law from buying each other drinks in many areas.

All the evidence seems to show that most families were slightly better off during the war – and a number were much more prosperous than they had ever been before. It was doubtless for this reason that there was a marked decline in the number of cases coming to the attention of the NSPCC. The Society still had to cope with an alarmingly high number of cases of cruelty by modern standards, but it was able to report in 1918:

> There never was a time in this country when there was less child neglect.

On the other hand, there was an increase in juvenile delinquency, caused by lack of parental supervision with the father in the Forces and the mother out at work.

49   A cookery class for mothers who have come along with their babies and small children. People became more socially conscious during the war and women who found it difficult to cope were helped in many ways.

11 Food and Rationing

Very few children went really hungry during the war and, in fact, some of them were much better fed than they had ever been before. But in those days, they didn't expect much in any case.

There was no fridge in the kitchen or freezer in the garage full of tempting food but only a pantry, sometimes damp, with a piece of bead-fringed muslin to keep the flies out of the milk jug and a wire-gauze dome to protect the meat. There were no supermarkets, with shelves crammed with food from all parts of the world, but only little shops with butchers in blue-striped aprons, fishmongers in straw hats and grocers in white coats. Many butchers had no ice-storage rooms to keep meat fresh over the weekend, and mothers and children would go out at night to one of the many street markets whose stalls were lit by naptha flames to get a cut-price piece of pork or beef for Sunday dinner.

Children from poorer homes had plain, stodgy, filling food – plenty of bread, marge and jam, porridge, dumplings, potatoes, bits of fat bacon, rice, semolina, and suet puddings, cut-price broken biscuits and an occasional treat of a kipper or a bloater – and the Sunday joint.

Children, on the whole, ate far fewer sweets than they do today. Sherbet, humbugs and jelly-babies were sold from glass jars or open boxes displayed on the counter, but most children couldn't afford to buy them more than once a week. Pocket money varied enormously, just as it does today. Sidney Offord, a London printer's son, and Rose Greaves, a Yorkshire vicar's daughter, were both born in 1908. She got ½d a week and he got a shilling (5p).

Richer children, for once, didn't do much better at the table than children from poorer families. Their parents might be downstairs gorging themselves on soup, fish, duck, fruit tarts and cheese, but the menu in the nursery was very different. The nursery-maid and the children sat down to a much plainer meal, though the children might persuade the cook to give them a special treat from the parents' table later.

Hoarding

Food didn't become really scarce in Britain until the war was nearly over, though fears of shortages led many rich people to hoard huge mounds of tea, sugar, rice, flour, condensed milk, tins of syrup and other food in their ample store cupboards during the first few weeks of the war. The price of a loaf of bread went up by a halfpenny, setting a profiteering pattern which was to continue throughout the war.

War bread

Towards the end of 1916, the government was becoming increasingly concerned about food supplies. White bread was banned, to economize on the use of precious grain and a new, standard, darker loaf was introduced. Later on, the bread became even darker, as barley, oats, rye, soya and potato flour were added. But bread, the staple diet of the poor, was never rationed.

			Age		
	Quality		Morning	Afternoon	TOTAL
	ORDINARY				
	NURSERY				
	HUMANIZED				
	STERILIZED				

MILK CHILDREN OR INVALID'S **PRIORITY CARD.** WINTER, 1917-1918.

me and dress of Dairy.

sumer's me and ddress.

ame of child or patient

Daily uantity f milk solutely cessary. **INTS**

octor's gnature Address

P.T.O.

50 A child or invalid's milk priority card.

U-boat campaign

In February 1917, the Germans started an unrestricted submarine campaign in which they sank all ships, including neutral vessels, on sight, in the hope of starving Britain into surrender. As shipping losses rose – from 540,000 tons in February to 870,000 tons in April – food became increasingly scarce.

But the government, not wanting to intervene, was just as reluctant to introduce rationing to ensure fair shares for all as it had been to bring in conscription. Children and invalids were given priority cards for the dwindling supplies of fresh milk and the production of sweets was cut back to a quarter of what it had been in 1915 to save sugar.

Empty shops and queues

The winter of 1917, which was exceptionally cold and wet, was the worst time for food shortages. Shopkeepers made customers buy other goods before they would sell them foods, like sugar, which were in short supply, even though this was unlawful.

Shops were often empty of goods, or opened for only an hour or two a day, and there were endless queues. The memory of those times is still vivid in the minds of people who lived through them. Alice Hancox (born 1897):

> I remember going to the butcher's for meat. My mother had died and I looked after the house. The people in the shop used to shout and argue that we were getting more than our fair share. They used to scream at me.

Women were convinced that the middle classes, those who could pay higher prices, and others who were friendly with the shopkeeper could get a little extra.

Rose Greaves (born 1908), the vicar's daughter, recalls:

> I must have waited in the queue for an hour or two with women in their shawls and clogs. Eventually my father came to get me and I remember the women saying, "EEE, parson gets in without waiting in queue".

Rich people, however, didn't queue. They still had ample supplies delivered to the tradesman's entrance, though butcher's boys were sometimes looted on the way.

◄ **51 In 1915 there was a National Food Campaign to make people more aware of the dietary value of certain foods. Here the bowler-hatted gentleman is instructing schoolboys on the nutritional value of various kinds of foods.**

Food control

Prices of food varied from one part of the country to another, but all rose alarmingly. Bacon cost 1/- (5p) to 1/6d (7½p) a pound. Eggs were 4d (2p) to 5d (2½p) each; chickens 2/6d (12½p) a pound; butter 2/- (10p) a pound. Price controls were introduced but they created an even bigger black market.

While Esme Strachey (born 1902) was at her boarding school fighting for the largest slice of bread and marge, things were not much better at the home of Rose Greaves, who was six years younger.

> You could only have one piece of bread. Occasionally, we had eggs. My mother made jam from swedes and flavoured it with something. We lived in a rhubarb-growing area so we had masses of that; but we had very little sugar so it was very sour.

Food rationing

There were so many angry scenes in queues and so many protest demonstrations by war workers and mothers that rationing was finally introduced in 1918. Sugar was the first food to be rationed on 1 January and, by the spring, half a dozen other foods had been included in the scheme.

Rations varied a little but the normal quantities for each person per week were:
Sugar: 8 ounces
Butter or margarine: 5 ounces
Tea: 2 ounces
Jam: 4 ounces
Bacon: 8 ounces, rising in July 1918 to 1 pound.

But there were still many queues for other foods, particularly at the butcher's. Meat was rationed by price and mothers had to register with one butcher. Some people still managed to get more than their fair share of meat, or at least avoid the queue. Sidney Offord (born 1908) remembers:

> When rationing first came in, my mother had been going to this butcher for a long time. He told her: "You don't want to stand in the queue with these people. You send

52   Rationing was finally introduced in 1918. Sugar was the first food to be affected and so people began seeking alternatives.

the boy on Friday night with your ration books." It was not at the butcher's shop, but at a house.

Food kitchens

To supplement the rations and to make up for shortages, food kitchens were set up in poorer areas in many parts of the country – takeaways where you had to bring your own metal cans, jugs or covered dishes. The Salvation Army set up food kitchens in very large towns. The food was usually sold in penny portions, though one kitchen provided a dinner for six people for 1/- (5p). This consisted of a large jug of soup, double portions of haricot beans and peas, and a whole boiled suet pudding large enough to cut into six portions.

The best customers were children and old age pensioners; the latter received 5/- (25p) a week when they were 70.

School meals

At the end of the nineteenth century, school meals were provided for poor children by some charities like the Cinderella Clubs which started in Bradford in 1892. By 1906 there were about 350 clubs of this kind throughout Britain. In that year, local authorities were allowed to provide school dinners out of the rates. By 1914, about 200,000 school children got free dinners, though they were not particularly appetising. In Tottenham, London, they got a chunk of bread, a bowl of pea soup and semolina pudding. But, by the end of the war, the number of school children on free dinners had fallen by 80 per cent – another indication of how the working classes had prospered during the war.

Food shortages in other countries

Although English mothers in the endless queues grumbled to their children, they were never as badly off for food as the Germans. There were violent food riots in Berlin in 1915 and meat became so scarce that Prussian Ministers advised people to eat crows instead. There were more riots after the failure of the

potato harvest in 1916. It was about this time that Zara Hershman was starving in Vienna.

Country people of all nations were usually less affected as they produced much of their own food. Raymonde Butcher (born 1900), who lived near the trenches in France says:

Being in the country, there was no shortage of food. We had chickens, a pig and our gardens. We used to go to the butcher when we wanted a change of food.

Coal rationing

Coal rationing was introduced in Britain in 1917 with 2 cwt (about 105 kg) a week for families with three to five rooms and 4 cwt (about 210 kg) for those with six to seven. Gas companies tried to persuade their customers to economize by boiling only the amount of water they needed and cooking as many dishes as possible in the oven at the same time. To save on precious fuel, Summer Time was introduced in 1916.

Petrol rationing

Petrol rationing was introduced early in the war and some cars were powered by a gas cylinder secured to the roof. But only a minority of rich people were affected by this shortage.

53 As food became scarcer, land was dug up in woods, on commons and sometimes even in village lanes, to become allotments. These schoolgirls have been collecting the vegetables which they have grown. These were sold to their parents and friends and the money was given to hospitals or charities.

12 Health

More than one in ten of all babies born in 1914 died before they reached their first birthday, most of them in the first three months. The main causes of death were wasting diseases, premature birth, bronchitis and pneumonia, and diarrhoea and enteritis. Even those children who survived the first year of life were not remarkable for their health. In some of the factory towns, many of the children entering school had ricketts, about one-third had enlarged tonsils and almost three-quarters had dental decay. Diphtheria, tuberculosis and scarlet fever were much more common than they are today. When these children grew up, their bodies still bore the marks of their deprived childhood. The medical examinations of wartime conscripts showed that less than three in ten were completely healthy and four out of ten were totally unfit for any form of service.

It is scarcely surprising that at that time men could only expect to live until they were 52, on average, and women until they were 55.

Improvements in health care
Although the infant mortality rate increased slightly during the first years of the war, so that it reached 105 per thousand births in 1915, reforms had already been introduced which were to help to bring it down to its present level of less than 20 per thousand.

In 1914, government grants enabled councils to set up ante-natal clinics, where women could get medical attention before they had their baby and advice on how to bring their child up afterwards. The first clinic had been opened in St Pancras seven years before. In 1917, the first National Baby Week was held to emphasize the importance of infant care. In towns throughout the country, mothers proudly pushed their perambulators in great parades. School children were asked to write essays about the Baby Week. One wrote:

> Every baby ought to be brought up with the same birth right but some are born right and some are born wrong. It is our duty to see that those who are born wrong are put right. (H.M. Walbrook, *Hove and the Great War*, Cifftonville Press, Hove, 1920)

School meals provided the poorest children with some nourishment and higher wartime wages and working mothers helped to give other children better meals. A school medical service had been started before the war in 1907, which ensured that all children received

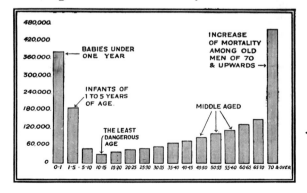

◀ **54 A chart showing the degrees of mortality at different ages. This was published in 1917 and shows that, despite the reforms, many children died before they reached their first birthday.**

some sort of medical examination three times a year.

Another important reform just after the war was the Housing and Town Planning Act of 1919 which gave local authorities subsidies to build council houses for the first time. As a result of this and later Acts, thousands of children moved out of one-room slums in crumbling unhygienic tenements into relatively decent houses and flats. After the Second World War, drugs were developed to cure and to prevent many deadly childhood ailments, such as polio and whooping cough.

Influenza epidemic

Unfortunately, no drugs were available to deal with the great pandemic of influenza which swept indiscriminately across the lands of allies, enemies and neutrals alike, from 1918 to 1919. Many schools were closed as the death toll rose. Some victims dropped dead in the streets; others had a more lingering death in bed. In all, about 150,000 people died in Britain. Rose Greaves (born 1908) had a particular reason to remember that period:

> My father said more people died in the parish from influenza than men were killed in the war. He had two or three funerals every day. My grandfather sent us a crate of oranges and my father made us have one every day. None of us got ill.

The victims included Leefe Robinson V.C. who had shot down the first airship over London. He had survived many aerial combats, being shot down over the Western Front by an enemy plane, and German captivity, but died in bed of influenza in December 1918. On the other hand, influenza saved Ernie Hancox (born 1900) from being conscripted:

> I'd had the 'flu, and the doctor wouldn't let me go, though I wouldn't have had to go in any case. I was due to report on November 14, 1918 and the war ended on November 11. I missed it by three days!

55 "Toothbrush drill" in a school in Swansea. Part of the government's health campaign.

56 Children being supplied with a mid-day meal at a canteen. The cost was 1/3d (6p) a week. The health of many poor children improved during the war because many of them were for the first time provided with proper meals.

13 Peace Celebrations

Final German offensive

After the revolution in Russia and her withdrawal from the war in 1917, the Germans were able to switch large numbers of troops from the Eastern to the Western Front. Their only chance of victory was to mount a huge offensive before the freshly trained, well-equipped American armies entered the war in force.

In the spring and summer of 1918, the Germans broke through the Allied trenches in several places and fanned out. They reached the River Marne again, threatening Paris, just as they had done at the beginning of the war; but, once again, the Allied line held, this time with American aid, and the Allies started to advance. There were heavy casualties on both sides. In Germany, civilians starved of food and fuel, were demanding peace. German sailors mutinied. In October, the new German Government started to sue for peace. The Kaiser abdicated on 9 November and fled to neutral Holland. An armistice was signed two days later.

Victory celebrations

At home, people watched the newspaper billboards as they had done in 1914, but with hope now, not horror. The end came more rapidly than they had expected. Special editions of papers were rushed out and excited newsboys shouted out the long-awaited news in the streets. Maroons and sirens sounded, no longer to warn of air raids, and church bells rang. Rose Greaves (born 1908) recalls:

All the mill sirens went off. We were in school and we were called up to the Assembly Hall and sang "Rule Britannia". Then we were sent home. My parents had gone to Bradford.

Someone gave me 6d (2½p) and I bought a flag. Everyone celebrated outside the Town Hall. The Mayor gave a speech and we all sang "God Save the King".

Many schools all over the country had a half-day holiday and excited children streamed out on to the crowded streets to join the adults, soldiers and civilians who were cheering wildly and waving flags. In Bristol, the *Western Daily Press* reported:

Above all, it was a children's day, for daddy had won the war. From the dainty tot richly attired to the rushing rag-a-muffin, who got in everybody's way, they were all in it.

Noteworthy was the inevitable band of kiddies, some without boots, headed by a large Union Jack and each one beating a tin can of some sort, which marched in orderly fashion four abreast up Clare Street.

But this was a day of victory and no less for the kiddies. As they moved on with their indescribable medley of noise, the arm of the burly police sergeant on duty there went up, and traffic stopped as the joyful youngsters passed.

The celebrations went on all night with huge bonfires being lit near effigies of the Kaiser dangling from gibbets. The celebrations in London were particularly wild with impromptu firework displays in every district.

Sidney Offord (born 1908) remembers:

57 A peace party organized for children and soldiers who had been wounded.

We were little devils. There was a firework called a cannon cracker. In those days, the lamplighter used to walk round the streets turning on the lights. They were gas lamps with a glass ball and a mantel. He used to push up the glass ball to stop air putting out the lights. One of us boys pushed a cannon cracker up. Just as it exploded a policeman came along.

But many people couldn't join in the celebrations. Tom Wills (born 1899), who was wounded in both legs towards the end of the war, was brought back to England in a hospital ship.

I went to a big house, owned by the Duke of Northumberland, which had been turned into a hospital. I was there on Armistice Day. My mother came to see me and she said there were soldiers everywhere, all climbing on the trams and buses and shouting and laughing.

Many others didn't like the raucous celebrations. Alice Hancox (born 1897) recalls:

We had some Canadian boys staying with us. They took us to Birmingham. It was a sight, absolutely packed with soldiers, climbing on buses and trams, shouting. I was very glad to get back home. The soldiers were singing at the tops of their voices.

In some places, the celebrations went on for days. The *Western Daily Press* reported:

In the daytime, school children from various parts of Bristol made the city lively at times and in the evenings, the streets were again crowded by young people of both sexes until a late hour.

Responsible citizens express the opinion that after four days of it, the thing might be given a rest.

But, in many homes, Armistice Day was overshadowed by the influenza deaths, the 2½ million war casualties and, particularly, those deaths which had been reported on Armistice Day itself. There were still thousands of the dreaded yellow telegrams to be sent out. Rose Greaves (born 1908):

Several men in our parish were killed that day or the day before. It was awful for those widows.

Peace

Like those widows, wartime children and teenagers had to carve out a new life for themselves in the changed conditions of the peace. They had mixed fortunes.

The Austrian refugee, Zara Hershman (born 1900) recalls:

58 Three weeks after the Armistice, King George V went to France to inspect the troops. British soldiers line the streets while the King talks to some French children who have given him flowers. The pretty white dresses must have been safely locked away for the four years of fighting or they would never have survived.

59 After the war the army found it difficult to recruit men. In order to attract people back into the forces they issued posters like this, showing the increased rates of pay since the beginning of the war.

After 1918 my father sent us money and worked hard to get permission for my mother and us to come to England. Eventually, he succeeded. I took a secretarial course at Pitmans in Southampton Row. For a whole year I never went to a cinema or concert or theatre.

My sister came to England later and started a business of her own: machine embroidery. I helped her. We did it in the bedroom. She borrowed money to buy two machines. Then she rented three rooms in Bishopsgate.

Herbert Bell (born 1897) became an assistant in an ironmonger's shop. He lost his job in the depression and was unemployed for a year. Sidney Offord (born 1908) never wanted to be a printer like his father; he worked on a small farm in Sussex as a young man and later owned a large farm of his own. Ernie Hancox (born 1900) who missed the war by three days,

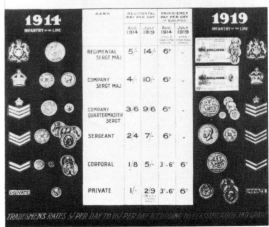

H.M.REGULAR ARMY
OLD AND NEW RATES OF PAY
COMPARISONS Nº II

	RANK	REGIMENTAL PAY PER DAY		PROFICIENCY PAY PER DAY IF QUALIFIED		
1914 INFANTRY OF THE LINE		Aug 1914	July 1919	Aug 1914	July 1919	**1919** INFANTRY OF THE LINE
	REGIMENTAL SERGT MAJ	5/-	14/-	6ᵈ		
	COMPANY SERGT MAJ	4/-	10/-	6ᵈ		
	COMPANY QUARTERMASTER SERGT	3/6	9/6	6ᵈ		
	SERGEANT	2/4	7/-	6ᵈ		
	CORPORAL	1/8	5/-	3ᵈ-6ᵈ	6ᵈ	
PRIVATE	PRIVATE	1/-	2/9	3ᵈ-6ᵈ	6ᵈ	PRIVATE

TRADESMENS RATES 3/- PER DAY TO 16/- PER DAY ACCORDING TO CLASSIFICATION AND GRADE

and became a 14-year-old chauffeur, lost his job. He says:

> After that, I worked in a private house as a gardener for 5/- [25p] a week. Later on, I went to Wales and drove charabancs.

Post-war promises

But, however much their individual dreams may or may not have come true, the promises made by politicians – "a land fit for heroes" "the war to end wars" "a million new houses" – were never fulfilled. There were some post-war reforms and improvements, however.

The Education Act of 1918 raised the school-leaving age to 14, but the most important part, providing for compulsory part-time education for young people of 14 to 18, was never carried out.

A million new homes were built by 1927 but most of them were private houses which ordinary people still could not afford to buy.

The Representation of the People Act 1918, gave the vote to all men over 21 and to women over 30 if they were rate-payers or wives of rate-payers.

The number of motor vehicles increased from 663,000 in 1920 to 2,287,000 ten years later but, even though the smallest car cost only £100, it was beyond the budget of most working people.

There were great improvements in health, which reduced the infant mortality rate from its pre-war level of 110 per thousand live births to 67 by 1930 and increased the expectation of life to 59 for men and 63 for women.

But the high wages of munitions workers and full employment did not survive the war. By 1921 there were over two million unemployed again and, although the numbers fell in the Twenties, they rose to new heights in the great depression of the Thirties. Unemployed men, some of whom had been wounded, shivered on cold street corners selling boxes of matches, with a crudely written placard tied by string round their necks saying "Ex-Serviceman". Was this the land "fit for heroes" which the politicians had promised? Neither was it the war to end wars. By 1939, the ex-servicemen's sons and daughters were fighting the Germans once again.

60 The scene outside Buckingham Palace on 19 July 1919, after the procession to celebrate peace. The war had been over for eight months, but there were few signs that the post-war promises of the politicians were going to be fulfilled.

Date List

1914   (28 June) Assassination of Archduke Franz Ferdinand and his wife at Sarajevo
(28 July) Austria declares war on Serbia
(29 July) Russia mobilizes 1,200,000 men
(1 August) Germany declares war on Russia
(3 August) Germany declares war on France
(4 August) Germany invades Belgium
(4 August) Great Britain declares war on Germany
(20 August) Fall of Brussels
(23 August) Battle of Mons
(6 September) Battle of the Marne begins
(December) First air raid over Dover
(25 December) British and German soldiers fraternize in no-man's-land

1915   (19 January) First Zeppelin raid, over Great Yarmouth and King's Lynn
(19 February to 15 March) Bombardment of Dardanelles by French and British battle ships
(18 March) French and British ships attempt to proceed to Constantinople, with loss of one French ship and two British; fleet retreats same day; 2000 lives lost
(April) Battle of Ypres
(7 May) Sinking of the *Lusitania*
(23 May) Italy enters the war

1916   (February) Battle of Verdun begins
(May) Conscription begins in Britain for bachelors

1916   (July) Battle of the Somme begins
(August) Battle of Paschendale begins

1917   (6 April) United States enters the war
(October) Russian revolution; they had suffered 5½ million casualties in two and a half years of war
(November) First major use of tanks on the Western Front
(5 December) Armistice between Russia and Germany

1918   (28 February) Food rationing begins
(March) Russia signs peace treaty with Germany
(March/August) Major battles on the Western Front
(1 April) Royal Air Force formed
(11 November) Armistice Day

Books for Further Reading

Anon, *A Soldier's Diary of the Great War*, Faber and Gurger, 1929
Castle, H.G., *Fire over England*, Secker and Warburg, 1982
Coppard, G., *With a Machine in Cambrai*, HMSO, 1969
Gibbs, Philip, *Realities of War*, William Heinemann, 1920
Herries, J.W., *Tales from the Trenches*, William Hodge & Co, 1915
Lansbury, George, *Your Part in Poverty*, George Allen and Unwin, 1917
Medical Officer of HM 23rd Foot, Royal Welsh Fusiliers, *The War the Infantry Knew*, P.S. King & Son Ltd, 1938
Metchim, D.B., *History of the War*, Arthur H. Stockwell, 1918
Peel, Mrs C.S., *How We Lived Then*, Bodley Head, 1929
Pankhurst, Sylvia, *The Home Front*, Hutchinson, 1932
Remarque, Erich Maria, *All Quiet on the Western Front*, Triad Paperbacks 1977
Taylor, A.J.P., *The First World War*, Penguin, 1966
Taylor, A.J.P., *The Habsburg Monarchy*, 1964
Thomson, David, *England in the Twentieth Century*, Penguin, 1965
Turner, E.S., *Dear Old Blighty*, Michael Joseph, 1980
Witkop, Philip, *German Students' War Letters*, Methuen, 1929

Glossary

AA	anti-aircraft guns; manufacture of these special guns did not begin until 1916; the first effective guns were borrowed from the French
balaclava helment	knitted garment covering the head and shoulders; first worn by British soldiers in the Crimean War, where the main base was Balaclava
bi-plane	early type of aeroplanc with two wings, one above the other
celanese	artificial silk
Cenotaph	memorial to the dead; from the Greek word, meaning an empty tomb
charabanc	early name for an excursion coach; from the French *char-à-banc*, a carriage with benches
conscription	compulsory period of military service; unlike the majority of European countries, Britain still does not have conscription

dogs-wool	wool which has already been used
frog	attachment on a soldier's belt for carrying a bayonet or sword
Huns	term of abuse for Germans; the Huns were an Asiatic race who invaded Europe in the fourth and fifth centuries
internment	keeping enemy aliens in camps during wartime; the biggest camp on the Isle of Man contained about 20,000 Germans and Austrians
Kaiser	or Emperor; Wilhelm II was Kaiser of the German empire from 1888 to 1918
kindergarten	nursery school; from the German "children's garden"
maroon	explosive device, giving a loud report, which was used in the latter part of the First World War as an air raid warning
monoplane	aeroplane with one wing
naphtha	a white spirit, which preceded paraffin, used in lamps
NCO	non-commissioned officer; a corporal, sergeant, or sergeant-major, who is in charge of private soldiers but does not hold a commission from the monarch, like an officer does
ninon	lightweight silk fabric
OTC	Officers' Training Corps, set up to provide grammar school and public school boys with some military training which would help them to become officers when they left school
pandemic	disease which affects many countries
putties	long strips of khaki cloth wound round the leg like bandages, for protection and support
rickets	children's disease which results in softening of the bone, associated with malnutrition
Royal Flying Corps	formed in 1912 and merged in 1918 with the Royal Naval Air Service to form the Royal Air Force
skivvy	domestic servant
suffragette movement	started in 1903 by Mrs Emmeline Pankhurst; it used direct action to get the vote for women
swagger cane	short stick carried by soldiers when walking out
Territorials	army of volunteers who did military training in their spare time to provide a reserve in case of war; formed in 1907 out of the former volunteers
U-boat	submarine; from the German *Unterseeboot*, "an undersea boat"

Ernie Hancox (born 1900) at 14, when he became a chauffeur

Acknowledgments

Alice Hancox (born 1897) at 15

1912

Herbert Bell (born 1897) in the army in 1915

Ann and Jack Vincent (born 1908 and 1905)

Sidney Offord (born 1908)

Raymonde Butcher (born 1899)

Rose Greaves (born 1908)

Tom Wills (born 1899)

Index